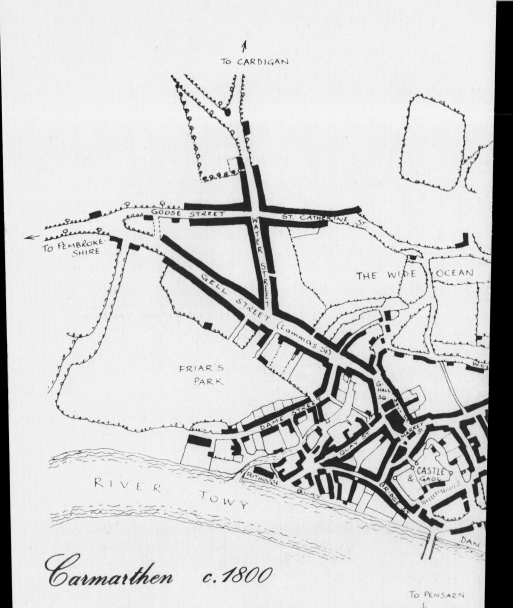

Carmarthen c. 1800

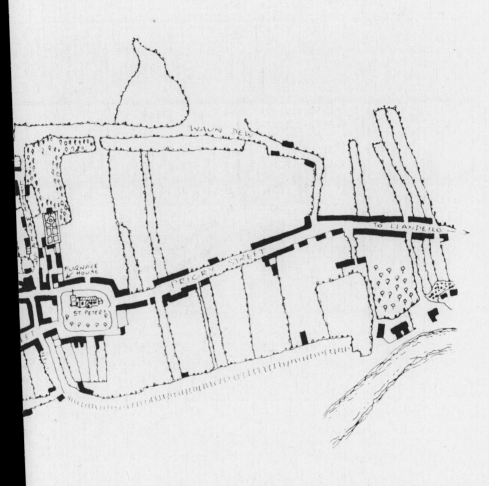

WAUN DEW

TO LLANDEILO

PRIORY STREET

FURNACE
HOUSE

ST PETER

PAT MOLLOY 1979

A Shilling for Carmarthen . . .
the town they nearly tamed

A Shilling for Carmarthen . . .
the town they nearly tamed

PAT MOLLOY

Pat Molloy Publishing

New Edition - April 1991

ISBN 0 86383 182 6

© 1980 Pat Molloy

Printed at
Gomer Press, Llandysul

To my wife, Hilda
and to
Michael, John and Anne

ACKNOWLEDGEMENTS

The author gratefully acknowledges the help given to him by the staffs of the Dyfed County Record Office, the Carmarthen Museum, the Dyfed County Library, the National Library of Wales, the Public Record Office at Richmond, and the British Library Newspaper Library at Hendon. He acknowledges, too, the value of source and background material derived from his readings of the local newspapers of the 19th century (the *Carmarthen Journal*, the *Cambrian* and the *Welshman*), of the Journals and Transactions of the Carmarthenshire Antiquarian Society, and of J. & V. Lodwick's "Story of Carmarthen" and its precursor, William Spurrell's 1879 study of "Carmarthen and its Neighbourhood".

Mr. Theo Rogers, lately Town Clerk of Carmarthen, is thanked for giving the author the benefit of his considerable knowledge of the town's history and for the loan of old books and photographs ; Mr. Raymond Rees, himself a Towy coracleman, is thanked for sharing his unrivalled knowledge of coracle family folklore ; and many other Carmarthen people, too numerous to be mentioned individually, are thanked for contributing so many stories and pictures of old Carmarthen.

INDEX

FOREWORD

"Local history is the only real history," my old tutor at Oxford used to say. He had a point. The great historians, the Gibbons, the Macaulays and their modern counterparts, can illuminate for you the major sweep of world events and the wars that change the destiny of nations. But all the time I am reading about the happenings in the limelight of History my mind keeps turning back to Wales, to the ordinary folk who had to struggle to earn their living from a harsh land and yet succeeded in snatching a little enjoyment out of life and even to distil it into poetry and music. "Never mind the Congress of Vienna or the Coronation of Queen Victoria," I mutter to myself, "None of our family were there. Tell me what they were doing in Pontarddulais at the time."

Fortunately we now have many distinguished local historians in Wales who have devoted themselves with skill and enthusiasm to the task of telling us what people were doing in Pontarddulais and elsewhere in Wales while the great folk were strutting and performing on the world stage. And fascinating accounts they are. But I've noticed one thing. Local historians tend to hurry over what I call "the seamy side". Perhaps the influence of the Methodist Revival still persists. We lack a ' News of the World ' view of History. There has been a gap in the true picture of Welsh life in the past.

And now that gap has been filled, for one town in Wales, by someone specially equipped for the task. Pat Molloy has written the story of the Police Force in Carmarthen during the 19th Century. In his book, *A Shilling for Carmarthen* he has presented us with a vivid picture of the night life of the ancient borough and of the policemen who did their gallant best to control a town that had the reputation of being the most wide-open town in Wales. The pages are packed with stories that would make the fortune of many a novelist. The author tells his story with wit and with understanding for the happy sinners of Carmarthen and for the guardians of the law who had to run them in, but who realised the temptations which beset them only too well.

Pat Molloy had one qualification for the task which no academic historian could possibly rival. He is the Detective Chief Superintendent of the Dyfed Powys Police force. Here at last you have a piece of local history written from the inside.

WYNFORD VAUGHAN-THOMAS

ILLUSTRATIONS

INTRODUCTION

This is a story of a hundred years of life in Carmarthen, the hundred years that saw the most far-reaching social upheaval in British history.

It begins in 1800 when Carmarthen, a thriving port and manufacturing centre in south-west Wales, had five times the population of Cardiff, a village sixty-five miles to the east. It ends in 1900 when Cardiff, the Capital City of Wales, had a population sixteen and a half times that of what had become a small west Wales agricultural market town, almost bereft of industry, whose handful of little coasters represented a maritime tradition soon to die.

It tells of the transformation of a violent, troubled and isolated town—a town with many of the characteristics of the Amercian western frontier—into a comparatively tranquil one, brought close to its neighbours by an unprecedented revolution in communications. Its leading characters are a body of men who played no small part in that transformation . . . the "New Police", created out of the shambles of medieval "Watch and Ward" and formed of a band of illiterate drunkards and gaolbirds who survived the kicks and curses of their fellows to hand to their more disciplined and respected successors the torch of a new concept of peace-keeping.

The story of Carmarthen's own tiny force of twelve coppers —the "Carmarthen Shilling"—is the story of the early tribulations of police forces throughout the Kingdom, where men such as these—wayward, hard to handle, no less drunken than the "lower orders" from whom they were drawn—created, sustained against all the assaults of a hostile populace, and handed to the 20th century, the substance of a police system second to none.

xiv

And since the story of policemen and police work must be set against the background of contemporary life, that of the "Carmarthen Shilling" reveals something else . . . the origins of Carmarthen's reputation as a town that still has one foot in an age when people were far more gregarious, far more hospitable, far more neighbourly, far less inhibited and far more convivial . . . so that we discover why Carmarthen is renowned, as far afield as Welshmen have travelled, as—well—a "different" town.

CHAPTER ONE

THEY CALLED HIM WIL ALONE

At a chill March midnight hour more than thirty years ago, a moment of history fleetingly and whisperingly touched a small, sleeping and silent Welsh town, and so soft was its whisper that it was heard by only one man.

It was one of those moments of history which more often than not pass unnoticed or unmarked—significant only in retrospect and, by the quiet manner of their passing, of no earth-shaking consequence anyway. And yet like many of them it held the key to a glimpse of the lives of identifiable people, in familiar streets, in generations past—people whose whole lives would otherwise disappear in the vast, anonymous mass into which conventional history casts the ordinary people who make it.

Sergeant Emrys Thomas heard history whispering to him as he sat alone in the old grey-walled police station in Carmarthen's Cambrian Place at midnight on the thirty-first of March, 1947. It whispered the end of the town's tiny police force, which at that moment ceased to exist as a separate entity.

The force passed away in silence, save for the slow ticking of the old wall clock in the charge room, with none of the customary ceremony, parade, church service or formal handing over of the custody of the town when the County force took over. Only Emrys Thomas marked this quiet end to what had often been a noisy and turbulent era of Carmarthen's history. As midnight struck he obeyed the last order given to him by Chief Constable Howel Evans earlier that night as he shook his hand and walked out of the station house into retirement. He reached up to the noticeboard and removed a piece of paper which bore a message from the Chief Constable to his little force, thanking them for the loyalty, service and respect he had received in his nearly thirty years in the borough and wishing them and their families good fortune for the future.

I

This simple gesture and this total lack of ceremony symbol-ised the reluctance of the Borough of Carmarthen to lose the force of which it was so proud, and whose one hundred and eleven years of existence had seen so much change in the shape of the town and the condition of its people.

And yet it was not always so. There was a time when the police in Carmarthen, as in the Kingdom as a whole, were reviled and physically abused by all classes of society—not excluding the "gentry"—who saw them as an instrument of oppression.

The force was born in 1836, at a time when Carmarthen, the most turbulent town in Wales, was as wild as any frontier town of the American west and run by one of the most corrupt municipal administrations in the Kingdom ; when destitution and disease plagued its labouring classes, and when a rioting mob was more likely to face a cavalry charge than a line of policemen.

It started life as a body of illiterate drunkards—many of them gaolbirds—whose only resort in the face of violent public contempt was sheer physical strength and yet, with the passage of time, it became one of the civilising influences which were to tame the town's wilder spirits.

The fact that for much of its existence it had consisted of its Chief Constable, two Sergeants and nine Constables, had led the townspeople to coin the term "The Carmarthen Shilling"—its twelve coppers—still spoken of in the town with affection and not a little nostalgia.[1]

But now it was over, and the old police station, which had seen and heard so much commotion over the years, was hushed as the ghosts of the old "Carmarthen Shilling" awaited to-morrow's influx of County policemen.

It was the end of an era. One of those quiet moments of history.

Emrys Thomas' thoughts during his lonely night's vigil might have drifted back over the years, back through the mist of time, to the ship-filled river of Carmarthen's maritime past, to the fighting fishermen and sailors, to the drinking, noisy, jostling, crowded streets of a busy market town, to a smaller, older, rich-and-poor town, to a time nearly a century and a half

2

before, when another solitary figure stood guard. For they say that at the beginning of the nineteenth century, when George the Third reigned, Carmarthen had only one policeman.

They say it was Wil y Lôn[2] who watched then, over a Carmarthen that was just beginning to break out of its medieval cocoon ; a cluster of stone buildings, huddled to ancient town walls, tumbling over each other, laced by winding steps, in a short, steep, drop to the river's edge and its ship-lined quay.

Wil y Lôn was a relic of the middle ages. He was a tattered remnant of a system of policing designed in a far-off age of tiny isolated rural communities and small, walled, market towns. He watched Carmarthen in a manner that had changed very little over the five centuries since 1285, when King Edward the First (who gave the borough its first Charter) put the maintenance of law and order into a formal framework called "Watch and Ward". Then the town gates had closed at sunset, leaving only the fool-hardy to face the perils of wolves and out-laws in the dark night world outside.[3] Then a "Watch" of twelve men patrolled the curfew-cleared streets and called to account those abroad without authority. Now, only old Wil met the 19th century requirement that—

> "None need apply for this ' lucrative ' situation that have not attained the age of 60, 70, 80 or 90 years ; blind with one eye, and seeing very little with the other ; crippled with one or both legs ; deaf as a post ; an asthmatic cough that tears him to pieces ; whose speed will keep pace with a snail, and the strength of whose arm would not be able to arrest an old washerwoman of fourscore ; whose constitution is worn out in hard service either in the army or navy."[4]

Wil y Lôn could neither read nor write. Too lazy to do "honest" work, he earned a few coppers for drink and a crust by walking the dark streets as a "Watchman" while honest Christians were abed, taking good care not to risk his neck by tangling with the fighting drunks who swarmed the quay and the meaner streets. And he had no police station ; only a small, unmanned, windowless building known as the "Roundhouse" in Cambrian Place, where he locked up any prisoners the magistrates might order him to take.[5]

Turning out from his cottage as dusk came, cloaked and muffled, with his watch-pole, lantern and truncheon, Wil would report to the Mayor, before lighting the oil lamps around the town. Walking the narrow streets, lanes, courts and passages among other lantern-carrying inhabitants, he watched the noisy streets empty of the last of the carousers well into the early hours, and then, carrying his lantern to light his way through the dark passages and across the pools of darkness between the few oil lamps in the Dark Gate and around Guildhall, Wil would call "Starlight, fair and all's well" on his lonely way through the little town. Fortified as many of his successors would be by surreptitious visits to the tiny ale-houses and gin-shops that abounded in the narrow streets, he would see the night through (huddled for most of it in one of his little "Watch-boxes"), extinguish the lamps and report to Mr. Mayor on the events of the night.

The loneliness of Wil's job inevitably prompted some wag to give a neat and appropriate turn to his name. And it stuck. They called him "Wil Alone".

Wil represented an ancient system of law and order that was falling apart. It was falling apart under the enormous pressures of the first decades of the 19th century, when the ending of the Napoleonic wars filled the country roads with desperate vaga-bonds; when towns burst at their seams as impoverished peasants deserted the countryside ; and when the formation of vigilante groups testified to the virtual collapse of law and order.

Carmarthen saw it all. There was no town in Wales so troubled so distressed and so destitute of law and order.

Here, the old system finally disintegrated under the hammer blows of the Reform crisis of 1831, when a beleaguered central government, its hands full of civil disorder and fearful of imminent revolution, responded to a cry of despair from Car-marthen's magistrates by sending a handful of London's "New Police" to face the notorious "Carmarthen Mob".

Until then, Carmarthen's watchmen would differ little in method, dress or effectiveness from old Wil Alone. And their beats would look, and sound and smell much the same as his.

4

It was a tiny old town. It was the home of around five and a half thousand people, crowded into no more than about four hundred houses, and it was just beginning to outgrow its ancient bounds. Little more than a stone's throw from its twelfth century Parish Church of Saint Peter, earthen roads left the huddled town behind, linking the last straggling thatched cottages in Priory Street with the village of Abergwili to the east, while, to the west, the track climbed over open country from a developing Lammas Street, to drop down into the village later to be named Johnstown,[6] over the Royal Oak Common where, until only a few years before, people convicted of felony within the Borough of Carmarthen were publicly hanged.

The River Towy formed the town's southern boundary, crossed as it had been for at least five centuries by the first bridge up from the sea and overlooked by the glowering grey bulk of the County Gaol, which for a decade had usurped the commanding position of the once proud castle, humbled by Cromwell. Beyond the river, the track followed the way of the Romans to the hamlet of Pensarn, and then went away south-eastwards to the beginnings of the industrial revolution in the South Wales valleys. It was at Pensarn, on Babell Hill, where now stands Babell Chapel, that felons convicted of crimes outside the Borough boundary were still publicly hanged, the corpses being taken back to the scenes of their crimes and hung on gibbets to rot away into grisly, rag-covered skeletons, as examples to others.[7]

But small as it was, Carmarthen was (paradoxically, given the lowly state of most of its inhabitants) a booming town—the social and commercial centre of the area. It was a thriving port, with ship building in its riverside yards, and its home-registered sailing vessels (more than sixty of them) shared the River Towy with ships from as far away as the Americas. Its iron and tinplate works exported to all parts of the world, Carmarthen tinplate being reckoned the finest in the Kingdom. Above all, it was—then as now—a busy agricultural market town. The country people flocked to the town with their carts, pack horses, mules and donkeys to sell their produce, and the farmers to hire their labourers, and all came to buy fish, cockles, oysters, woven Welsh wool, the shoes and beaver hats for which Carmarthen was famed, and a host of other locally produced wares. They came from many miles around, and thought nothing of walking the round trip of nearly sixty miles from as far afield as Cardigan or Llandovery just to visit the markets. The removal of the old Dark Gate a few years before had opened a narrow passage between broad, cobbled Lammas Street and the town's bustling centre above and below the Guildhall, an area packed with stalls and shacks which were scarcely passable on market days. Hawkers shouted their wares, and the tall, black hats of the country women bobbed among a thousand heads. Tradesmen in their broad-brimmed top hats, tailed coats, knee breeches and buckled shoes, hurried about their business through crowds of rag-covered, shoeless peasants and dirty, noisy, running urchins. Country gentlemen, pantalooned, cravatted, side-whiskered and bewigged, closed the windows of their beleaguered, crowd-pressed coaches to protect the delicate senses of their ladies from the noises and smells that swarmed around them. Cattle, horses and pigs edged through the dense crowds, herded by their drovers to the fairs in Lammas Street and Priory Street, adding to the crowds of people, animals, carriages and carts that pressed into the narrow, incredibly filthy, earthen streets of the little town.

Near Dark Gate and the Guildhall, large crowds thronged the streets and every possible vantage point to watch bulls tethered to iron rings fixed in the ground, being baited by Carmarthen's celebrated bulldogs, doubtless keeping a respectful distance from the animals in the knowledge that the landlord of the Boar's Head Hotel had been killed by one of the bulls in Dark Gate. At the Market Cross above the Guildhall,[8] others found amusement in abusing the unfortunates clamped in the stocks, and in Spilman Street they would flock in their thousands to look up to the scaffold high above the gaol walls for the public hangings, amid such excitement and in such a wild, carnival atmosphere that the authorities not suprisingly wondered whether their intended deterrent effect might not be outweighed by the disorderly behaviour of the mob which

6

packed the streets and Castle Hill. It was as good a spectacle as a Tombstone or Dodge City lynching, and there was none better than the last of them. In September, 1829, around ten thousand people watched this most bizarre of all the town's public executions. They saw David Evans, of Llanfihangel Rhos y Corn, close to Brechfa (about fifteen miles from Carmarthen), pinnioned and blind-fold, fall through the trap door —taking the broken gallows crossbar with him ! The startled man thanked God that he had "survived the first death", which, in common belief, meant that he would be spared. But he couldn't have been more mistaken, and "the workings of the despair upon his soul were indicated in the gloom that overcast his countenance"[9] as he was dragged, pleading for mercy, to be "launched into Eternity" from the hastily-repaired apparatus of death.

There were, of course, many other entertainments in the town. There were grand balls in the coaching inns, of which the last, the Boar's Head, still stands to-day with its narrow coach-wide entrance in Lammas Street. They resounded until the early hours as the gentlemen and better class of tradesmen vied with their inferiors in the amount of drink they consumed. It was a truly noisy, boisterous town, which knew how to enjoy itself, the gentry dancing until dawn and the "lower orders" filling the town's countless ale-houses and gin-shops, and all taking noisily to the streets together, throwing fireworks, rolling blazing tar barrels, brandishing flaming torches and firing pistols in the air whenever there was a change of monarch, an election or a famous victory to celebrate.

That was how they celebrated in Carmarthen as the bells of Saint Peter's Church heralded the year 1801 and a new century ; as they shared man's age-old delusion that the movement of the clock past the magic hour of midnight would bring an end to all their troubles and the realisation of all their different aspirations. They could not know what a long, hard road lay ahead.

But at least Carmarthen was embarking on her era of prosperity—that relatively short-lived zenith as the most populous town in the Principality which preceded her slow but steady decline as the centre of Welsh gravity shifted further and

7

further eastward in the wake of the industrial revolution. The town was bursting out of its medieval bounds in a blend of Georgian elegance and suffocating squalor, as country gentlemen, made rich by the demands of the Napoleonic war, built their town houses and tradesmen built their warehouses and workshops, while the "lower orders" crowded more and more of their families into tiny, dark houses under the pressure of the most rapid increase in population Carmarthen would ever know.

It was in the tightly packed riverside hovels—in Chequers Alley, Pump Row, Cotterill's Lane and Justice's Lane, on the Quay, in Dan y Banc and Towyside, and in Goose Street and Water Street—that the seamen, fishermen, coraclemen and labouring classes of the town were to be found. They lived four and five families to a tiny house and seven or eight people to a tiny room, with one bed and one blanket between them, often in unbelieveable poverty and distress,[10] for the facts of early nineteenth century life were that there was a huge and virtually unbridgeable gulf between the rich and the emerging "middle-class" on the one hand, and the labouring poor on the other.

At the turn of the century, too, almost a third of Carmarthen's inhabitants—some one and a half thousand—depended for their livelihood on fishing the river and the sea, and the seasonal nature of their trade and the lowly state of their existence created such instability as to ensure that the fishermen and coraclemen would for many years yet be found in the forefront of the mobs which so often terrorised the town.[11]

For the poor in those distressed times, living in filth and disease and in abject poverty, there was no way out. Small wonder that the "lower orders" sought solace in drink, with all the social consequences that followed. Drink was cheap and abundant in Carmarthen's grog-shops, which numbered about one hundred and fifty, in a town of a little over five thousand people. Drunkenness and its attendant domestic strife and public brawling were ever-present features of life in Carmarthen until well into the present century.

Perhaps it was inevitable that since the "Watchmen" and later the policemen of the early nineteenth century came from the "lower classes" of the community, they would exhibit the

8

They called him Wil Alone

Carmarthen . . . a tiny old town

The New Market, 1846: "... a very handsome one, which will bear comparison with any in the Kingdom"

Carmarthen Quay, 1830

same traits, and so it was that many of Carmarthen's first policemen were every bit as drawn to the jug as their labouring brothers, as we shall see.

The very few who were willing to watch the streets of Carmarthen in the early years of the nineteenth century were old, illiterate, drunken men who were too lazy or unfit to do "honest" work, and the town's "constables" (appointed under the Charters) were burgesses for whom the title carried merely the status of corporate office, with no semblance of a police function. As late as the eighteen thirties, even the Chief Constable was little more than the supervisor of the Watch . . . in between attending to his own business.

The magistrates (of whom the Mayor was chief in the borough) were the key figures in the field of law and order. It was they who faced the mobs and called upon the troops in the all too frequent moments of desperation;[12] they who investigated and prepared criminal cases for the courts ; they who dealt with minor offenders brought before them by the Watchmen. The relationship between the Mayor and the Chief Constable can be likened to that between the Mayor and the Sheriff of any American frontier town in the hey-day of the Wild West.

But the Mayor was a politician. He was the leader of the town's corporation, and if Carmarthen possessed many of the characteristics of a wild American frontier town, its political justice smacked equally of the naked corruption of the worst of nineteenth century American local politics. Witness one paragraph from the report of the Parliamentary Commission on Municipal Corporations in England and Wales, published in 1834 :[13]

> "The municipal government of (Carmarthen) is mainly carried on for political purposes and with a view to securing the political interests of the prevailing party. This object is pursued throughout : in the election of Mayor, Sheriffs and Common-councilmen ; in the appointment of Gaoler, Constable and Bellman ; in the choice of Magistrates and Juries ; in the application and management of the Corporation funds."

Even that arch-exponent of the art of municipal graft and

corruption, Mayor Richard Daley of Chicago, could hardly have earned a more eloquent testimonial !

And yet it would be wrong to see the Carmarthen of those days only as a soulless centre of materialism, violence and drunkenness, because these were also the times when the enlightenment of the later, Victorian, period began to flicker through the dark hopelessness of the poor masses. Social consciousness, beginning as a patronising charity towards the poor ; political consciousness, beginning as a philosphical belief in equality and democracy ; and moral consciousness, manifesting itself in the non-conformist rejection of established religion in favour of movements with a more popular appeal, all made their appearance in Carmarthen. The town had for centuries provided the best available in education to the fortunate few ; its long-established grammar school produced a steady, though very small, stream of talent and Carmarthen would always be in the forefront of educational innovation in the years before compulsory education began to open the door of opportunity to the masses. A Mechanics' Institute, a Musical Society, a Literary Society, a theatre, anti-slavery and anti-drink meetings exemplified the town's cultural and moral stirrings, while the rapid expansion of religious activity and the flurry of church and chapel building in the town in the early years of the century played a most significant part in transforming the moral and social conditions of the town by that century's end.

For all this, though, it was its reputation for violence— encapsulated in the term "The Carmarthen Mob"—that earned Carmarthen its name as the most turbulent town in Wales. In an age of political and social unrest, of drunkenness and destitution among the "lower orders", of extremes of wealth and poverty, and of the disintegration of medieval "Watch and Ward", Carmarthen led the field.

Through to the eighteen thirties, the crisis years, the years that saw the birth-pangs of the "New Police", old Wil y Lôn and his like, and the embattled Carmarthen magistrates, fought their losing battle. It was a battle that was to reach its climax in 1831.

NOTES

[1]It was a 12-man force from 1857 to 1939, when, with the outbreak of war, the strength was increased to 16. But it continued to be known as "The Carmarthen Shilling".

[2]Trans : Wil the Lane, a reference to his calling.

[3]The last of the old town gates, the King Street Gate and the Dark Gate, were pulled down in 1792.

[4]A satirical view of 19th century Watchmen in "The London Charleys ; or half past twelve o'clock and a very cloudy sort of morning" by John Pearson, published in London in 1827.

[5]The first roundhouse was erected in 1804 and the Cambrian Place site was thereafter continuously occupied by lockups, gaols and police stations until 1956. The foundations of this historic site now lie under yet another supermarket.

[6]After John Jones, M.P., of Ystrad (1777 to 1842), of whom we shall hear much more.

[7]The last to be hanged there was a preacher. Rees Thomas Rees had killed his lover by administering a potion intended to procure an abortion. His preacher's eloquence served him well as he prayed before a crowd of ten thousand and exhorted them to "beware of temptation" before being "launched into Eternity". He was hanged on 19th April, 1817.

[8]The site of the market until 1846, when the new market ("a very handsome one, which will bear comparison with any in the Kingdom") was opened on the drained marshland known as the "Wide Ocean". That market, though shorn of its original grandeur through a century and a half of neglect, was as busy as ever when it fell to the hammer of modernisation in 1980.

[9]*The Carmarthen Journal.*

[10]This description could be (and was) applied to the town in 1873 by the public health inspector, who described a town of cess-pools among buildings standing on land sodden with centuries of human waste, and of open sewers and drains. The severe overcrowding and the insanitary state of the poorer sections of the town even then made Carmarthen a breeding ground for contagious diseases—with the highest death rate in the kingdom !

[11]Food riots occurred regularly in the first two decades of the century and elections would turn the town into a battlefield. The "Carmarthen Mob" earned Carmarthen its reputation as the most turbulent town in Wales.

[12]In 1757, Mayor John Evans ordered troops to fire on a mob of colliers ransacking a corn store. Five were killed—and the Mayor was tried for Murder ! He was acquitted.

[13]National Library of Wales.

CHAPTER TWO

A PLACE IN HISTORY

The early eighteen thirties were watershed years for Carmarthen. Caught up in the fever of agitation for electoral reform, the town was to experience violence on such a scale as would overwhelm its pathetically inadequate "police" and cause the government to send in officers of the recently formed London Metropolitan Police, backed by the army. They were years that would see Carmarthen take a place in local government and police history by being branded as the most (though by no means the only) politically corrupt borough in the whole Kingdom, in a report which led to the wholesale reform of municipal government and the creation in the cities and boroughs of police forces modelled on the London Metropolitan Police, formed six years earlier by Sir Robert Peel.

As if this were not enough history making, Carmarthen was to set another record. Only once in Welsh history did the "King's Writ" for the holding of a Parliamentary election fail to be enforced and that dubious honour fell to Carmarthen in the "Reform" elections of 1831.

Altogether quite a distinction for a small, remote, market town !

But first, the agitation for electoral reform which, to many, seemed about to plunge the country into revolution. Until the reforms of 1832, political power in Britain was in the hands of a governing class consisting of the aristocracy and the landed gentry; it was political power based on the ownership of property by both those who sat in Parliament and those few whose votes and patronage sent them there. "County" families held parliamentary seats almost as of right, and there was no subtlety about the dispensation of their favours, since seats were openly offered for sale right up to the passing of the Reform Bill in 1832. Some seats even had firmly established market prices—

in pounds if the buyer was of the same political colour as the seller, in guineas (5% more) if he was not !

Open, public balloting (the secret ballot was not introduced until 1872) served to ensure that all manner of inducement and even intimidation could be brought to bear on the small electorate. A most glaring example of the former was the attempt in 1802 by Sir William Paxton, the London banker, to bribe the Carmarthenshire voters by spending nearly £16,000 on wining and dining them. In this extravagant two-week campaign, which became famous as "Y Lecsiwn Fawr" (the Great Election), Paxton paid for 11,070 breakfasts, 36,901 dinners, 684 suppers, 25,275 gallons of ale, 11,068 bottles of whisky, 8,879 bottles of porter, 460 bottles of sherry and 509 bottles of cider. He even promised to pay for a new bridge over the Towy if he were elected. Carmarthen's inns and ale-houses were awash with free drink, and in what must have been one of the greatest hangovers ever, the Carmarthenshire electors cast their votes . . . and rejected their benefactor ! In a fit of pique, so the legend goes, Paxton spent the money he had earmarked for the new bridge on building the tower now known as Paxton's Folly, which, from its high hill just up river from the town, commands a most magnificent view of the beautiful Towy valley. But perhaps he found some small consolation in being elected Mayor of Carmarthen in the year of his defeat.

As to intimidation, imagine having to register your vote aloud, in the presence of vociferous political antagonists, in the jury-box of the Guildhall, outside which a howling, stone-throwing, partisan mob is kept at bay only by the bayonets of the Militia, and you have something of the flavour of a nineteenth century Carmarthen election.

If the parliamentary vote could be won by inducement and intimidation, political power in the government of the borough of Carmarthen could be (and was) manipulated through the burgesses, whose ranks were packed with the relatives, servants and friends of the ruling "County" families. As we shall see, the report of the parliamentary commission bore eloquent testimony to all the forgery, fraud and corruption by which this was effected.

13

Against this background, the emotion with which the Reform movement was charged, and the strength of the opposition to it, might suggest that the intention was to give the vote to the masses. This was far from being the case, but what the Reform issue did was to provide a label to which the masses could pin all their grievances—poverty, unemployment, the scarcity and the high cost of food, harsh laws and vicious punishment ; in fact all the debit side of the industrial revolution.

And in Carmarthen there was additional fuel for the fire . . . the fishermen and others of the "lower orders" who comprised the notoriously exciteable and volatile "Carmarthen Mob", ready as always to latch onto an excuse for a punch-up.

THE RED AND THE BLUE

The names of two of Carmarthen's streets—Red Street and Blue Street, which meet at the junction of Guildhall Square and Dark Gate—are the last echoes of the struggles for political power which gave the town its out-standing reputation for violence in the eighteenth and early nineteenth centuries. The Guildhall and its square were the battleground.

While ostensibly representing the political factions of Tory and Whig, the colours were really the emblems of the two dynastic factions which dominated Carmarthen's county and borough politics in the years before Reform. They were powerful family groupings formed by the houses of Dynevor, Golden Grove, Edwinsford and Cwmgwili—the Rices, the Vaughans, the Campbells (Earls of Cawdor), the Williamses and the Philippses—who owned vast estates and properties in the counties of Carmarthen, Cardigan and Pembroke. Parliamentary seats in the counties and in boroughs such as Carmarthen were for generations held by or, almost literally, through the gift of, these ruling dynasties, whose power also extended to every part of local administration and, through the magistracy, to the administration of justice.

To say that political passions ran high in Carmarthen is to make a monumental understatement. For a hundred years before the Reform riots, Carmarthen's parliamentary and local government elections had turned the town and its Guildhall into a veritable battleground, as the party that happened to attract the following of the "Carmarthen Mob" terrorised the borough's few voters. The election of 1796, for example, saw a man wounded by a pistol shot and buildings barricaded against the savagery of the mob, who roamed the town setting fire to and attempting to demolish the houses of any who were known to support the other side.

Every succeeding election in the borough was hotly contested and left its trail of broken bones and windows. Over the several days it took for the voters to go to the Guildhall and publicly declare themselves, there would be uproar, the Militia would stand to (where they were not actually called into action by the Mayor), and dozens of special constables would be sworn in to augment the few, near-useless "regulars".

There was no better example of this than the "Reform" election of 1831.

If The Streets Should Flow With Blood

By 1831, John Jones of Ystrad,[1] lawyer and one-time protégé of the Blue house of Cawdor, had been the Member of Parliament for the Borough of Carmarthen for ten years. Now a Red and a vigorous opponent of Reform, he fought the seat in 1831 against the Whig, Captain John George Philipps, R.N., of Cwmgwili, veteran of Nelson's battle of the Nile, whose father had represented the borough from 1784 to 1803.

While less than five hundred of the borough's twelve thousand or so inhabitants would decide the issue by the vote, the far more numerous "Carmarthen Mob" would dictate the temper of the campaign, and they were for John George Philipps and against John Jones, who had had their support in all his previous fights. The mob's defection on this occasion was due to John Jones' opposition to the Reform issue, which aroused expectations of democratic rights far beyond those actually intended, carrying an emotional campaign to the point where the very survival of the British Government (of Jones' party) was hanging by a thread.

Even without Carmarthen's tradition of election violence, there was good cause for apprehension that this election might be an explosive one, but Mayor David John Edwardes saw fit to rely on his "regular" policemen . . . part-time Chief Constable James Evans, brightsmith and zinc worker, and part-time watchmen David Rees, David Woozley, Thomas Thomas and David Morgan—who took time off from their jobs as labourers for the occasion.

The Guildhall doors opened on the morning of Friday the 29th of April, 1831. The Town Clerk and the candidates' check clerks, including John Williams on behalf of John Jones, took their places under the bench of Sheriffs, to begin the election proceedings. As the burgesses assembled near to the jury box through which they would pass to announce their preferences, the public seats and aisles filled with non-voting spectators.

James Evans and his men stationed themselves about the hall, though more as ushers than as men strategically placed for trouble.

The preliminaries over, John Jones began his address to the electors. Suddenly the hall was invaded by a large and noisy mob, and there was immmediate pandemonium in the packed chamber as the mob put Jones' supporters, the returning officers and the other corporation officials in fear of their lives. From his raised bench, John Williams, Jones' check clerk, had a grandstand view of the mob's entry into the hall, in the seconds before he was himself engulfed in the yelling sea of fists and boots. In his own words[2]—

> "After John Jones Esquire and John George Philipps Esquire had been put in nomination, there appeared in the hall a very numerous assemblage of persons acting in concert together as an Organized Mob, and conducting themselves in a tumultuous and riotous manner, menacing and threatening all who might come forward as voters for John Jones with the infliction of immediate vengeance. And one John Woods, who was one of the

persons acting in the Mob, struck me several violent blows with his fists in the immediate presence of the returning officers of the Court. I also saw a person named Charles Baron Norton strike John Jones a violent blow with his fist without any apparent cause whatsoever, and the Mob so assembled became so tumultuous and riotous in the Court that it was impossible for the Sheriffs to proceed in the business of the Election, and they were obliged to adjourn the Court to the following day."

Morgan Thomas, a magistrate, found himself in the customary situation of having to confront—and even hold off—the mob himself, without there being a constable in sight, they being lost in the heaving crowd :

"I immediately jumped down on the table and opposed myself to the mob, endeavouring to persuade them from further advance. One Morgan, son of a shoemaker, called out 'Let us kill him'. I fully believe that if opposed they would have put this threat into execution."[3]

The "police" were, of course, physically overwhelmed, but their hearts were not in it anyway. The Chief Constable and his men were terrified, as shown by Evan's own evidence (written the very next day) that—

" . . . if it became necessary to apprehend any person in the town for riotous conduct he could not effect it, and would be in danger of his life if an attempt were made, and that he does not believe that any of the Constables would act, and that the town and hall are in a state of Riot."[4]

So the election had been forced to a close. But the mob did not disperse. They roamed the town in groups, brandishing weapons of all kinds, attacking anyone suspected of being prepared to vote for John Jones, and besieging their homes.

For the rest of that day and well into the night, Mayor Edwardes and his fellow magistrates—now in a state bordering on panic—scoured the town for men willing to be sworn in as special constables to face the inevitable riot when the Sheriffs tried to reopen the election on the morrow. The "respectable inhabitants" kept well out of the way and those who could be found flatly refused to be sworn. In the event, out of some hundred and forty men approached, seventy-five of the "lower orders" were dredged from the streets of Carmarthen and sworn in before the Mayor.

And so Saturday dawned. The town was already full as shortly after eight o'clock James Evans, his four "regular" constables and his ragged band of seventy specials entered the Guildhall through the side door in Market Street. It was market day, and the streets around the hall resounded with the clamour and bustle of the stalls, the country people, the horses, pigs, carts and waggons which crowded into Guildhall Square and Upper Market Street.

The events of the previous day and night had served notice on the townspeople of exciting events to come, so Guildhall Square itself saw an early addition to the market crowd in the shape of a growing assembly of the "lower orders" come to see and to take part in the fun. John Woods, David Woolcock, John Evans of the Ball Court and a dozen other leading troublemakers were in the front of the crowd, waiting for the doors of the hall to be opened at nine o'clock.

Inside the hall, Chief Constable Evans made his dispositions, as the Sheriff and others concerned in the election proceedings took their places and arranged their papers. Seventy-five policemen covered the court room and its approaches and, given the size of the place, it might be imagined that, armed as they were with truncheons, they would have presented a formidable deterrent to would-be trouble makers. Enough has been said already, however, to show what such a body was worth when the chips were down, and Carmarthen was now about to see the clearest demonstration yet of the truth of it.

The front doors of the hall opened just before nine, and the crowd poured in. If he did nothing else that day, Chief Constable Evans made a note of the ringleaders inside the hall.[5]

Once again, the chamber was plunged into uproar and confusion as Friday's riot was repeated. John Williams, the Check Clerk, was again a prime target of the mob, who called out to

18

him to "quit the hall". John Evans of the Ball Court shouted
to Williams that—

> " . . . if he would not quit the (record) book and get
> out of the hall, that he would take away his life."[6]

John Williams declared that this inflamed the mob to such a
degree that he "was obliged to quit the hall to save his life".
He went on to say that he heard—

> " . . . several of the mob declare that if anyone came
> on to vote for Mr. John Jones that they would kill him,
> and the Mob appeared so determined in their purpose
> that the persons assembled at the Hall to vote for John
> Jones were deterred from offering their votes for him,
> and most of them were on that account obliged to quit
> the Hall, and the Sheriffs could only receive three votes
> for John Jones before they were obliged to run away and
> quit their post."

Morgan Thomas, the magistrate, again in the forefront, witnessed a slanging match between the parties at the centre of the
affair. Cries of "Resign, resign", addressed by the Blues and
their mob to John Jones and his supporters punctuated the
punching and kicking, and a climax was reached when George
Thomas of Ferryside, an attorney in the town and a fiery Blue
champion, made an "inflammatory" speech, calling on the
mob—

> " . . . to mark every person who voted for Mr. Jones
> and to show them that they were marked by giving
> them three hisses. As soon as Mr. Picton had voted,
> the Jury Box by which Mr. Jones' voters came up to the
> Poll was assailed by the mob, who forcibly possessed
> themselves of it. Their success was hailed by cheers
> by the mob in the Hall."[7]

The Reverend Edward Picton, brother of the town's hero,
Lieutenant General Sir Thomas Picton, who was killed at
Waterloo received none of the respect normally due to the cloth.
As the mob seized possession of the jury box with himself inside
it, Morgan, the shoemaker's son, seized him and roared—

19

"Your brother's Soul is in Hell, and your's will be there soon. Your brother fell in battle for his country. Come and fall here. We'll kill you !"[8]

One-eyed Samuel Rees was also prevented from casting his vote which he had intended to give to John Jones, because—

" . . . John Evans (of the Ball Court) who was active in the mob declared most vehemently that if I should give my vote at the election for John Jones he would *instantly poke out my remaining eye from my head*, so that I considered my life would be in real danger if I had voted for John Jones, and I was on that account deterred from giving my vote."[9]

This time there could be no excuse that the police were insufficient in number to make some show of strength, but they failed dismally. Those who did not run away with the Sheriffs either hid elsewhere in the hall or otherwise refrained from doing their duty. As the Mayor wrote later to the Home Secretary—

"Seventy special constables were sworn in on the 29th of April last during the violent disturbance which occurred at our election. That force we found not only inefficient but perfectly useless, as we imagine, from their close connection with the townspeople."[10]

He was right. Both mob and constables were drawn from the same class of people, so it was impossible for Carmarthen to contain such disorder as this from within its own resources. Now totally demoralised, its Chief Constable, James Evans, made no bones at all about his inability to cope with the situation. The magistrates took down his evidence that—

"The Hall was then filled with a very numerous mob, who conducted themselves in so tumultuous and riotous a manner that he was intimidated from acting in any manner against them. He and the other Constables present were quite unable to suppress the tumultuous conduct of the mob and he believes that if he had attempted it, it would have been at the risk of his life."[11]

20

Once again His Majesty's Writ had failed in Carmarthen. There can be no question but that the Mayor would have called on the military to restore order, but the Militia were out of town and the nearest garrison was at Brecon, fifty miles away.

So, for the violent weekend that followed, Carmarthen was virtually defenceless.

Having twice frustrated what they must have known would have been a Red victory, the Blues were cock-a-hoop. John Evans, John Woods, David Woolcock and the others led a huge, cheering crowd through the town, waving flags and banners, to the accompaniment of a band . . . and carrying a beaming Captain Philipps above their heads in a small boat !

It was triumph indeed. But it was anarchy, and the "respectable" inhabitants of Carmarthen lived under this reign of terror for many days.

Final confirmation of the Blue "victory" came with the extremely short-lived proceedings of Monday the 2nd of May. The hall did not open until one o'clock, and it quickly became apparent that everyone in the firing line had had enough. The "police force" had disintegrated, the Sheriffs and their officials kept away, and there was no sign of John Jones and his followers. Only Captain Philipps, George Thomas, the attorney and his most vociferous supporter, and a string of other supporters, and the Mob—ready to go again—were there in force to savour the moment.

The Sheriffs were sent for, but refused to come, so the Blue triumph was complete, and a rowdy dinner lasting well into the early hours at the Boar's Head Hotel rounded off Carmarthen's defiance of the King's Writ.

THE KING'S WRIT SHALL RUN

It was a rare event even in the early nineteenth century for the King's Writ not to run in a part of his Kingdom and for a town's authorities to admit total defeat in the face of public disorder. Indeed it had never happened before in Wales, and such a state of affairs demanded some kind of explanation to the government. So the magistrates of the borough wrote to Lord

21

Melbourne, the Home Secretary, on Sunday the 1st of May, 1831, giving a general statement of the unruly state of the town and asking for military aid.

So violent was the disorder during the remainder of that weekend and the final attempt, on the Monday, to hold the election, that the Mayor was obliged to despatch a further plea for aid only two day later. This time there was a note of real desperation :

> "The undersigned Magistrates are convinced no Warrant of any description can be enforced in the present state of the town without further aid, and are convinced that if one were to be captured and placed in Prison, the demolition of the Prison and the escape of the Prisoner would inevitably ensue, unless a Military force were stationed in the Town to overcome the Rioters."[12]

Within a couple of days, soldiers of the 93rd Regiment (the Argyll and Sutherland Highlanders) had force-marched to the town from Brecon. Their presence in the town was sufficient to overawe the mob. The reputation and the bayonets of those kilted and bonetted redcoats had the town quiet before many days had passed.

With the soldiers in the town and with the spread of the word that the magistrates were only waiting for the opportunity to employ them in rounding up the riot ringleaders, those gentlemen—seventeen of them—knocked on the thick, studded doors of the Borough Gaol in Cambrian Place and gave themselves up to the gaoler.

What happened next shook even the "respectable" people of the town.

Whereas the law required (and still requires) prisoners to appear in open court to be remanded on bail or in custody on properly formulated charges, the Blue rioters were examined behind the closed doors of the gaol by the Red town magistrates. Inevitably, bail was refused and they were locked in the cells.

The prisoners themselves must have been stunned by their treatment, but even though justice was in this case tainted, it was effective. Robbed of its driving force, the mob soon ran out of steam, and by the third week in May the borough authorities found themselves able to allow the troops to return to Brecon Barracks.

By the 28th, the magistrates felt secure enough in their authority to grant bail to the seventeen alleged rioters. And Carmarthen was restored to a state of riot.

Waiting for them as the gaol gates were opened was a huge crowd, most of them sailors, fishermen, coraclemen, boatmen and others of the "lower orders" who constituted the "Carmarthen Mob". The "Blue Seventeen" were paraded in triumph through the town, to the accompaniment of gunfire singing, chanting, and the sound of breaking glass.

Once more powerless, with neither police nor soldiers to help them, the magistrates again appealed to the Home Secretary for military aid.

It should be borne in mind that the army was already heavily committed in the major cities of England and in Welsh towns like Merthyr, where industrial unrest compounded the political situation. So this time the Carmarthen magistrates were curtly told that the policing of Carmarthen was the responsibility of neither government nor army. It lay squarely on their magisterial shoulders. The law made ample provision for the swearing in of as many special constables as were required to deal with any contingency and the whole male population of the town could be compelled to act if the magistrates had the strength to use their authority.

Those in Whitehall could hardly be expected to imagine the kind of people who comprised the greater part of the inhabitants of Carmarthen—distressed, starving, illiterate and, now, disaffected. So the disorder continued.

But that was only part of the problem. That the political violence was merely an addition to the normal state of disorder in the town is seen in the fact that while the Blue mob rampaged through the centre of the town—

> " . . . a tremendous affray took place on the Quay between an immense assemblage of fishermen and the proprietors of a Seine or large net used for fishing. The fishermen succeeded in tearing the net to fragments

23

and bearing it away in triumph. During the affray a gun loaded with shot was fired by one of the defensive party and wounded one of the assailants." (C.J.)

This was just one incident in a feud between the coracle fishermen of Carmarthen and the net fishermen of Ferryside and Llanstephan (on the Towy estuary) which spanned generations and which is part of the folklore of their descendants to this day.[13]

But back to the political struggle. On the 8th of June, desperation showed through a further appeal to the Home Secretary from the Mayor and magistrates :[14]

> "It is our duty to inform your Lordship that our population consists of about twelve thousand persons, the great majority of whom are in extremely poor circumstances, and the principal inhabitants have shewn an unaccountable degree of apathy.
>
> The streets have been paraded nightly by a Mob of several hundred who have done considerable mischief and under these circumstances we feel assured that no constabulary force can preserve the peace of the Town.
>
> We therefore again humbly request your Lordship will assist us by sending a Military force to our aid."

But the government remained firm ; the borough must look to its own resources for its day-to-day peace-keeping. Military assistance would be made available for a specific and non-routine contingency on the giving of adequate notice. Thus the magistrates were forced to recruit bands of "specials", who proved totally useless in the face of the continuing riots in the town. The magistrates could not even get the truncheons back from those who ran away, as the Mayor explained to the Home Secretary :[15]

> "Twenty-four staves of office were delivered out to the Special Constables on the occasion of the (unspecified) riot, which the Chief Constable has been directed to collect, and he reports to me he is unable to get in more than six."

The violence reached its climax on the 10th of June, when a noted Pembrokeshire supporter of Reform visited the town, to an enthusiastic reception by Whig supporters. As the Mayor reported to the Home Secretary[16]—-

> " . . . a procession was got up to receive the Hon. Dr. R. F. Greville, on which occasion the persons who were committed by the Magistrates for riot and who paraded the Town with music and banners after their liberation, again paraded the Town wearing badges with the words *"Persecuted Reformers"* printed on them. Great confusion ensued. On neither occasion had I the means of re-pressing them.
>
> My Brother Magistrates and myself feel convinced should any opportunity for riot occur, lives will probably be lost. We are conscious of having done our duty in representing the state of the Town to His Majesty's Government, and having done so, we cannot believe ourselves responsible for the future peace of the place."

In other words, the total collapse of authority in the town.

On the 29th of July, 1831, the "Blue Seventeen" surrendered to their bail at the Carmarthenshire Assizes in the Guildhall to face charges of Riot, and there followed another example of the way in which even Justice in Carmarthen was tainted by politics.

Counsel for the defendants, instructed by George Thomas, their attorney (of the 'inflammatory' election speech), discov-ered that they were before a Grand Jury made up of "Red" burgesses. This jury, whose duty was to say whether or not there was a *prima facie* case against them for formal trial by a "Petty" jury, inevitably found that there was. So they had been committed for trial by "Red" magistrates, examined by a "Red" Grand Jury—and were now to be tried by a "Red" Petty Jury !

Defending counsel pleaded with the Judge on the manifest injustice of the whole affair, and His Lordship ordered the case to go before a jury chosen from men living outside the borough—a "County" jury. That jury—

25

" . . . unhesitatingly returned a verdict of acquittal, on the announcement of which peals of applause resounded through the hall." (C.J.)

Once again the "Blues" had triumphed, and there were more noisy processions through the town.

But it could not last. The House of Commons could not allow Carmarthen to remain unrepresented, so a new Writ was issued, and the magistrates were once more faced with the prospect of a violent election.

The new election was to take place on Saturday the 20th of August, so, in accordance with the stand the government had taken in June, the magistrates gave the Home Secretary clear notice that they could not cope with the expected disturbances. The government responded by posting cavalry and infantry to Llandeilo—a troop of the 14th Dragoons and the 98th Regiment of Foot—and by sending to Carmarthen six officers of the two-year old London Metropolitan Police Force. Being outside their area of jurisdiction, it would be necessary for the latter to be sworn in as special constables for the borough.

Having the time to look around, the magistrates swore in a number of townsmen as "specials," but took the precaution of swearing in a much larger number of Llanelli and Pembrey colliers to put some back-bone into the force they were assembling. The mine-owners were "Red" supporters, as, of course, were the magistrates, so the force of sixty-one "specials" was largely composed of men who would lose their jobs if they showed any favour to the other side !

And there was still the discredited Chief Constable, James Evans, with his four feeble "regulars", but they and the rest were put under the command of the senior of the London policemen—John Lazenby, Superintendent of London's Marylebone Division.

And so the battle-lines were drawn . . . for the "Blue Seventeen" were back on the streets of Carmarthen.

August the 19th, Friday, the day of publication for the *Carmarthen Journal*, and the day before the election was due to begin. The newspaper, noting the proximity of the army and the secondment of the London policemen, reported that—

" . . . we have no apprehension that the occasion should arise for their employment."

Indeed, everything about the town that day suggested a quieter than usual approach to an election. The busy streets were full of people intent only on the business of the day—the market stallholders and their haggling customers, the drovers, coaxing their cattle and pigs through the town, farmers and other visitors on horseback, amid the constant press of carts, carriages, waggons and coaches squeezing to and fro along the narrow, crowded streets. For the coaching inns Friday was a busy day, as people came and went before the weekend was upon them. The ostlers and porters plied a particularly busy trade at the Boar's Head and the Ivy Bush, and it was at the latter hostelry that the London coach arrived in the late afternoon, to be met by Mayor Edwardes and some of his fellow magistrates, including Daniel Prytherch.

They were there to greet six cloaked, high-booted, military-looking men who stepped down from the coach and introduced themselves—John Lazenby, Samuel Culwick, Dale Hubbard, William Thomas Turner, Samuel Hughes and John Davidson, officers of the London Metropolitan Police. Porters took their luggage to their various lodgings, while police officers and magistrates walked along King Street, through Upper Market Street and into the Guildhall, where the Mayor lost no time in administering the oath of office required of Special Constables in the Borough.

There followed a discussion on the peace-keeping strategy for the election period, including the strength of the forces available and the police deployment around the hall for tomorrow's proceedings. And then the officers were taken to their lodgings to change into their uniforms of blue, high-stocked, button-through tail coats, white 'duck' trousers and black tall hats . . . and to buckle on their truncheons and pairs of flint-lock pistols. These men had faced rioters before.

Evening came, and the six uniformed officers, with a party of "specials", were shown around the town by magistrate Daniel Prytherch, but the noise of shouting and gunfire from the direction of Spilman Street soon told them that rioting had already begun. As they turned into Spilman Street, near to the County Gaol, they met the mob, and John Lazenby, out in front, was—

> " . . . recognised as one of the London Police. He was assaulted and struck by a man with a club in his hand whilst he was attempting to put down the riot that was occurring there, and the mob assembled seemed to express their feelings with great warmth against him, and the mob then attacked the other five Police Constables who had accompanied him from London, together with Special Constables, and pelted them with heavy stones.
>
> In apprehending some of the principal actors in that Tumult, Dale Hubbard, one of the Police Officers, received a severe wound under one of his arms, which in great measure incapacitated him from being able to do any active duty as a Constable for two days after. And some of the Town Constables were also hurt on the same occasion, and the Town continued in a very disturbed and agitated state for a considerable time after. And large bodies of men and boys paraded the streets with the apparent intention of being bent on some mischief."[17]

Throughout the night the mob rampaged through the town, again seeking out their political opponents, but now far more intent on attacking the police, particularly the "London Thief Takers", who were to receive a good deal of punishment before this election was over. It was well into the early hours before the streets were cleared, the prisoners secured in the lock-up house, and the London Police, now reduced to five by Hubbard's injury, were snatching a little sleep before returning to the fray.

August the 20th. Saturday. Market day again, and the first day of the election of a Member of Parliament for the Borough of Carmarthen. The scene was almost as before—Sheriffs and officials in their places, voters assembling near the jury box, and the candidates and their friends ranged each side of the voting area. The force of some seventy policemen were stratically placed around the hall in groups, for mutual support. The leading potential troublemakers were now well-known and thus well marked by the police in the hall, so the proceedings opened in a much less disorderly fashion than in the previous April.

Speeches from both sides were loud, vociferously supported, and pulled no punches, and when the Sheriffs declared a preliminary show of hands to be in favour of Captain Philipps there was a particularly noisy outburst as an "individual present made a very offensive observation to the Sheriffs".[18] Unfortunately for posterity, the words used were not recorded ! At any rate, the proceedings were then adjourned until Monday morning.

The election occupied four and a half days, closing at noon on the Thursday, and becoming more rowdy each day. On the Monday—

> "The party supporting John George Philipps expressed their feelings in so noisy, violent and turbulent a manner that several of them were ordered by the Sheriffs to be put out from the Hall because they were interrupting the proceedings at the Poll. In taking some of such persons into custody for assaults committed on them, a general attack was made upon the Police Officers, with a view of rescuing from them those whom they had apprehended. The attack made was so determined and forcible that *the police officers were compelled to threaten the immediate use of their firearms*,[19] and had they not so acted, the consequence would most probably have been very serious, as many of the rioters were armed with sticks or clubs, which they had carried about them on the preceding days, and in many instances had made use of them in attacking and resisting the Constables in the execution of their duty." (C.J.)

Monday evening was lively too, as—

29

" . . . a large mob paraded through the public streets of the Town avowing vengeance to all who might oppose them, and threatening the lives of the Police from London." (C.J.)

By now the Mayor sensed very serious trouble, and fearing the consequences of the delay involved in the army marching the fifteen miles from Llandeilo, he called on the Royal Carmarthenshire Militia to stand to at their depot in Magazine Row—just five minutes double-quick march through Lammas Street to the Guildhall.

The Guildhall was particularly noisy on the Tuesday, but the mob had evidently been deterred from resorting to physical violence by the determined stand of the police and the arrests they made on the previous day. Lazenby described how—

"Mr. George Thomas, an Attorney, and the apparent principal manager on behalf of John George Philipps Esquire, addressed the assembly in a very inflammatory speech, and animadverted with great acrimony upon the London Police Officers being brought down to Carmarthen, and stated that John Jones deserved every insult that could be offered to him, and desired every one might do so, and that he was deserving of vengeance for sending for the London Police Officers, whom he described as the "London Thief Takers", and for sending for the colliers from Llanelli to trample down the free and quiet inhabitants of Carmarthen, and asserting that Mr. Jones had said that the streets of Carmarthen should flow with blood sooner than he should give up the contest, and also stating that soldiers were ready at Llandeilo to Dragoon and Bayonet the quiet and peaceable inhabitants of Carmarthen."[20]

George Thomas continued in the same vein next morning (Wednesday) and declared, in the manner of the powerful court orator he was, that he had only to say the word and the mob behind him would clear the hall. There was a time when George Thomas' word would have been the father to the deed, but John Lazenby and his men were proving a real deterrent. It did not happen, and no fists flew that day.

The evening was another matter. The mob roamed the streets once again, and—

> " . . . some panes of glass were broken in the window of Mr. David Jones, a Banker and Magistrate, who supported John Jones, and one young man and some Special Constables were violently assaulted and attacked by a mob opposing Mr. Jones in the public streets of the Town." (C.J.)

Day by day John Jones had been piling up the votes, and by mid-day on the final day, Thursday, he was in— by a majority of 71 from a total vote of 479. The victorious John Jones emerged from the hall, to be chaired in the traditional manner by "hundreds of his friends". Suddenly, the packed square exploded into violence, when—

> " . . . he (John Jones) was pelted with stones and was severely wounded on the forehead and blood flowed profusely from the wound, upon which several persons were taken into custody by the Constables, who were wounded and beaten most severely by the rioters, and one of the London Police Officers named Samuel Culwick was so wounded and beaten with clubs and stones that if timely assistance had not been given him no doubt his life would have been taken from him. And the Chief Constable of the Borough, Mr. James Evans, was also at the same time attacked by the mob and severely maltreated, and many more persons also received violent wounds from the mob on that occasion."[21]

By this time the battle was being fought in narrow Dark Gate, and as John Lewis Rees, a known supporter of John Jones, tried to approach the area on horseback to join the many other horsemen in the procession—

> " . . . being opposite or near the Guildhall, he was then and there violently assaulted by John Thomas, labourer, and by his brother, Thomas Thomas, barber, who laid hold of him and pulled him off his horse and then beat and kicked him in a violent manner without any the least provocation whatever."[22]

31

As for John Jones, the new Member of Parliament—

> "He soon regained his self-possession and was escorted by hundreds of his friends to Ystrad, where he alighted from his chair and congratulated them on the splendid triumph they had that day achieved by their firmness and their disregard of the system of terror which had been employed to intimidate them in exercising their elective franchise.
>
> Mr. Jones was too unwell to dine with the gentlemen who had supported him, who, to the number of fifty, sat down to an excellent dinner at the 'White Lion'. A great number of the burgesses, supporters of Mr. Jones, dined at different other inns of the town. The gentlemen of the Blue Party dined at the 'Ivy Bush'."
> (C.J.)

It is tempting to see John Jones as a battered and beleaguered champion of order, and his opponents as having the monopoly of violence and bad language, but this was not entirely so. Consider, for example, an incident a year later, by which time "Reform" had been passed into law by an embattled House of Lords, after perhaps the most serious and threatening political crisis of the century. John Jones was still probably the most unpopular man in Carmarthen, and—

> "On Saturday (the 13th of October, 1832), as P.G. Jones, Esquire, Solicitor of Carmarthen, was proceeding along Upper Market Street in that town, he was met and accosted by John Jones, Esquire, the present Member of Parliament for the Borough, who, producing a paper, asked Mr. P. G. Jones whether he was the author, to which Mr. P. G. Jones replied in the negative.
>
> Mr. John Jones, after embellishing his phraseology with 'Scoundrel, liar' &c., struck Mr. P. G. Jones violently, grappled with him, and was proceeding in full work when friends interposed.
>
> The combatants separated and Mr. John Jones was taken away, amongst the groans and hisses of all assembled." (C.J.)

32

John Jones had even been known to have recourse to the duelling pistols to back an insult to a political opponent, and he had shown that he could face a pistol muzzle with cold courage. But for now, in the summer of 1831, he was on the receiving end and nursing his wounds at Ystrad, while, out in the streets, John Lazenby and his seventy men fought the still rampaging mob and managed to arrest about half a dozen of the ringleaders. During the running battle—

> " . . . a prisoner was rescued (from one of the London Policemen) by the mob, who cut the policeman's head with a large stone and laid open his cheek with a bludgeon, the blow from which stunned him for some time. Chief Constable Evans was also violently assaulted and his head laid open." (C.J.)

The violence of this election reached a climax that afternoon, when—

> "Not satisfied with the outrage committed on the person of Mr. Jones, the Radical Mob paraded the town preceded by a band of music and a black flag on top of a pole. When they arrived at Saint Peter's Church they forced it open and several of them rushed up the steeple and tore down the flag which surmounted it in honour of Mr. Jones' election, and threw it down, amid the yells of the mob below.
>
> The old Sexton, who is about seventy years of age, jealous of the honour of his flag, made a desperate effort to recover it and succeeded in getting hold of the flagstaff, which he clung to, and was dragged a considerable way by the mob, many of whom were armed with treenails[23] which they held over his head and, using the most dreadful threats, succeeded in taking the bare pole from him, for in the scuffle the flag had been torn to tatters.
>
> In the course of the afternoon another flag was hoisted instead of it, and the mob again succeeded in breaking into the Church, but were not able this time to reach the belfry, for the ringers had armed themselves with formidable weapons and posted themselves on the staircase, and the assailing party seeing the determined man-

ner in which they were likely to be met gave up the
project and began demolishing the gas apparatus in
the Church.

Fortunately, the police came up in great force at the
critical moment and the perpetrators of these outrages
consulted their safety in flight. Several, however, were
secured and lodged in prison." (C.J.)

Although sporadic violence occurred for a few days more,
the police were winning and the streets were gradually being
cleared of the "Mob". And all this without resort to the Militia
or to the troops standing to arms in Llandeilo.

The final act took place next morning when the arrested
rioters were taken from the lock up and hauled up before the
magistrates in the Guildhall, where they—

" . . . behaved with the most audacious effrontery.
One of the parties pushed his fist in a Constable's face.
The magistrate upon this ordered his removal to prison,
when he became furious and layed about most desperat-
ely. He was, however, eventually secured and lodged
in prison." (C.J.)

John Lewis Rees, pulled from his horse and so badly beaten
the day before, was in Court to prosecute his assailants, Thomas
Thomas and John Thomas. The two were committed to gaol
and resisted in a most furious manner. John Lazenby and a
fellow London officer, William Thomas Turner, were dragging
the Thomases away when one of them kicked Turner so violently that he was totally disabled and dangerously ill for the remainder of his stay in Carmarthen.

But that was really the end of it and four days later things
were back to normal ("normal" in peace-keeping terms mean-
ing that the drunken violence in Carmarthen was now non-
political and confined to the "lower orders"), so the magistrates felt able to reduce their force accordingly. But, writing
to the Home Secretary on the 6th of September,[24] they hinted
at further trouble on the horizon :

"We think it necessary to retain Police Officers Lazenby and Davidson till after our Charter Day, which

will be on the 3rd of October next, when the elections of the different Corporation Officers are expected to be warmly contested and serious disturbances may be apprehended, unless an adequate force be provided for the preservation of the public peace."

CHARTER DAY

Daniel Prytherch had good reason to regard the approaching Charter Day with trepidation because it could fairly be called Carmarthen's annual "free-for-all" . . . a regular opportunity between Parliamentary elections for a bit of "Red versus Blue", for the West Wales Dynasties fought as fiercely over Carmarthen's Corporation as they did over any parliamentary seat.

Charter Day[25] was the day set by King George the Third's 1764 Charter for the election of the "Corporate Officers"— Mayor, two Sheriffs, six Magistrates and Chamberlain. They were elected from and by the burgesses, the only people with the vote in those "pre-Reform" days. Since the holders of the elected offices held the key to power in the borough—power over the lower courts, power to hire and fire everyone from bell-ringer to Chief Constable, and power over all the borough's assets—the intensity of the power struggle can be imagined.

Given the violent history of Charter Day and the demonstration only seven weeks before this one of the value of strong, well-planned peace-keeping measures, the magistrates again swore in a number of "specials", this time, it seems, *all* from the "Red" owned Pembrey collieries. But, as we shall see, they were marked men in the eyes of the mob, who now looked for revenge for the events of August.

The mob, too, was ready, and this Charter Day would see the police, battered and bruised, scattered to the four corners of the town, while the red-coated Militia fixed bayonets on loaded muskets to keep the mob at bay.

On the morning of Monday the 3rd of October, 1831, then, the burgesses assembled at the Guildhall to elect their officers, John Lazenby's police, in small pockets around the chamber,

35

were lost in the crowd that pressed into the seats and aisles of the public gallery and into every other vacant square inch of the Guildhall as the proceedings began. What happened during those proceedings was described by the *Carmarthen Journal* of the following Friday ; there was—

"A spirited contest, which in the course of the day terminated in the election of Mr. Daniel Prytherch as Mayor, by a majority of 33, the numbers being for Captain John George Philipps 175 and for Mr. Prytherch 208.

Just before the close of the poll, a most disgraceful and brutal attack was made on the constables by the mob, in the Mayor's presence. The constables were necessarily scattered in different parts of the court, and this gave their assailants from their immense numerical superiority great advantage over them, and they were obliged to fly, after having their batons wrenched from their hands and employed against themselves. We saw several thrust out of the hall, and some tremendous blows inflicted on them, and they were obliged to consult their safety in flight.

Mr. Lazenby, the Head of the Police, was very severely punished in endeavouring to quell the riot and was obliged to quit the hall, when he was again assailed and forced to take refuge in one of the neighbouring houses.

Things at this juncture appeared so serious that the magistrates called out the Staff of the Militia, under the command of Adjutant Banks-Davies, and they remained under arms in front of the hall until the close of the day's proceedings.

In that excited state of public feeling it was not deemed prudent to proceed with a contested election that evening, and the court adjourned to the following day to enable the authorities to take adequate measures for the maintenance of the public peace." (C.J.)

Battered and bruised though they were, the police eventually rallied, to seek out and lock up some of the ringleaders of the

Guildhall affray and to spend a busy night harrying groups of stick-carrying, window-breaking men and youths about the streets of the town. The Militia remained under arms, and received the same orders for the morrow.

Meanwhile, the magistrates put all their energy into bullying, threatening, cajoling and otherwise persuading any man they could find into being sworn as a special constable. Those colliers still unscathed from Monday's battle—and even some of the "walking wounded"—were pressed into service for Tuesday, and were deployed by John Lazenby that morning in a much more effective fashion when the Guildhall opened for business again. This time—

> " . . . public tranquility was preserved and the business of electing allowed to proceed without further interruption.
>
> We cannot too emphatically deprecate the system of terror which is attempted to be established by the agency of the mob to overawe and deter the timid from the honest exercise of their franchise, but we trust that the arm of the law, as in the present case, will ever be found sufficiently powerful to crush every attempt at intimidation, from whatever quarter it may come." (C. J.)

That trust was for the most part well placed. The "arm of the law" had prevailed, and Carmarthen gradually returned to normality. For the remainder of 1831 the only disturbances outside the usual run of drunken rowdyism arose from a politically-inspired campaign—occasionally backed by the "Carmarthen Mob"—against the payment of market tolls, but they were capably handled by the five "regular" and two London policemen, with the military always, and yet conspicuously, in the background.

NOTES

[1]The western suburb of Carmarthen, in the neighbourhood of his home, was named "Johnstown" after him.

[2]John Williams' deposition : P.R.O., File HO 52/16

[3]Morgan Thomas' deposition : P.R.O., File HO 52/16

[4]James Evans' deposition : P.R.O., file HO 52/16

[5]John Williams' deposition : P.R.O., file HO 52/16

[6]John Williams' deposition : P.R.O., File HO 52/16

[7]Morgan Thomas' deposition ; P.R.O., File HO 52/16

[8]Ibid

[9]Samuel Ress's deposition ; P.R.O., File HO 52/16

[10]Letter dated 8th June, 1831 ; P.R.O., File HO 52/16

[11]James Evans' deposition : P.R.O., file HO 52/16

[12]Letter dated 3rd May, 1831 : P.R.O., File HO 52/16

[13]See "The Ebbing Tide", Chapter 8

[14]Letter dated 8th June, 1831 : P.R.O., File HO 52/16

[15]Letter dated 21st June, 1831 : P.R.O., File HO 52/16

[16]Letter dated 21st June, 1831 : P.R.O., File HO 52/16

[17]John Lazenby's deposition : P.R.O., File HO 52/16

[18]*Carmarthen Jaurnal*.

[19]Author's Italics.

[20]John Lazenby's deposition : P.R.O., File HO 52/16

[21]John Lazenby's deposition : P.R.O., File HO 52/16

[22]John Lewis Rees' deposition : P.R.O., File HO 52/16

[23]"Treenails" were pieces of oak used in shipbuilding. "About sixteen inches long and one in diameter, admirably calculated for concealment under a coat to be used as a missile or a baton " (*Carmarthen Journal*, 26th August, 1831).

[24]P.R.O., File HO 52/16

[25]The first Monday after Michaelmas day, early in October

CHAPTER THREE

SOMETHING RESEMBLING A POLICE FORCE

So the violent year was over, and Carmarthen came out of it with a new Chief Constable and something now resembling a police force. John Lazenby's exertions during the riots had earned him the respect of the "better class" of townspeople and an invitation, which he accepted, to stay in Carmarthen as Chief Constable when his fellow Metropolitan policeman, John Davidson, returned to London. He does not seem to have made any formal arrangement with his "parent" force, though, because he was dismissed from the Metropolitan Police (for absence ?) in 1834. Though superseded by Lazenby, James Evans stayed with the force for another two years, as one of the four constables who were still employed on a year-to-year basis. The two of them were to face at least one more episode of political violence together before James Evans ceased to be a constable.

The Charter Day of 1832 was a particularly violent one, an occasion for riot, gunfire and military action, but it also saw the sensational arrest of a leading "Blue" by the "Red"-controlled police, and a petty piece of political justice meted out by the "Red" magistrates.

The election of the corporate officers passed off peaceably enough for a change, with the election of Grismond Philipps as Mayor and William Rogers and Thomas Davies as Sheriffs. It was afterwards that the streets began to fill up with marauding groups of partisans, and the "Blue" supporting mob did their usual tour of the town seeking out the homes of known "Reds" for suitable treatment.

In attacking the Star and Garter public house in Spilman Street,[1] though, they were taken by surprise when the landlord opened fire and sent several blasts into the crowd from his horse-pistols. As people fell wounded, the mob became more violent as the landlord reloaded and fired again and again.

39

The mob smashed the windows, pulled at the frames, hammered the stonework and set about pulling the building down around him.

Murder was in the air as the helpless police strove to get through the screaming mob to the besieged Star and Garter. But help was at hand. The Mayor had called out the troops, whose muskets and bayonets cleared enough of a path to the ravaged pub to allow him to confront the mob and read out the proclamation from the Riot Act : "Our Sovereign Lord the King chargeth and commandeth all persons being assembled, immediately to disperse themselves . . ." They also enabled Jonn Lazenby and his men to seize a few of the rioters, including some of the wounded, and to assuage the fury of the mob by arresting the landlord of the battered Star and Garter. The commander of the troops managed to persuade the leaders of the mob to lead them away from the scene, and accepted their condition that the troops should march away in the opposite direction.

One of the people engaged in the parley, on the "Blue" side, was George Thomas, the attorney who had been in the thick of the election battles of the previous year, and who had so successfully defended the seventeen "Blue" rioters. On this occasion, though, George Thomas made a serious tactical error. He was still in Spilman Street an hour after the Mayor had "read the Riot Act"—a hanging offence ! The police pounced. Not on George Thomas, for the moment, but on a young man named Henry Moss, who was put in the lock-up with the others. George Thomas was being saved for later —a wise move in view of the temper of the mob in Spilman Street.

CARMARTHEN JUSTICE

There was consternation in the town when the "Red" landlord of the Star and Garter, charged with shooting and wounding several of the mob, was freed ; when Henry Moss was refused bail, and, above all, when George Thomas was arrested, locked up and committed in custody to the Assizes. All this was done by "Red" magistrates, before whom—

"... bail was refused, although tendered by several highly respectable gentlemen to any amount. Neither was he then allowed to bring forward a single witness on his own behalf or to cross-examine those against him, the depositions of the latter being taken in rooms inaccessible to the accused being merely read over to him." (Cam)

A heavily subscribed petition was sent from the town to the Home Secretary—

"... condemning the conduct of the magistrates as arbitrary and partial, and praying a full investigation into the case." (C.J.)

Within a week, Mr. Justice Patterson in the High Court in London had issued a warrant commanding the Carmarthen magistrates to take bail for the two men. Their application before his Lordship was strongly contested on behalf of the magistrates, but the Judge scornfully dismissed their objection, saying that—

"He never heard of a more gross case and could not conceive of how any Justice could commit a respectable gentleman to prison for feloniously demolishing a house when it appeared on the statements of the witnesses for the prosecution that *all the damage was done before he got there.*"[2] (Cam)

A fast coach brought the Judge's warrant to Carmarthen, and the magistrates complied at once. And then—

"Immediately upon the intelligence being communicated to the town, crowds of gentlemen, tradesmen and others waited at the Borough Gaol (in Cambrian Place) and after the required bail had been duly given, formed themselves in procession and escorted Mr. Thomas and Mr. Moss to their respective homes amidst the loud cheering of many thousands who had assembled to greet their deliverance. Indeed, so spontaneous and marked an expression of public opinion was never before equalled by the inhabitants of Carmarthen." (Cam).

The trial and acquittal of the two men at the following Carmarthenshire Spring Assizes occurred in circumstances we have encountered before ; a "true bill" was found by a jury of "Red" borough burgesses, but the prisoners successfully applied to be tried by a jury of country people. And they were acquitted. This trial was cited by the 1834 Parliamentary Commission as a prime example of "political justice" as dispensed in Carmarthen.

It may be only an idle reflection, but if London had been not two hundred, but two thousand miles away from Carmarthen, as Washington D.C. was from Tombstone, Arizona, in the frontier days—who knows ? Carmarthen might have had its own version of "Lynch Law", because Riot was a hanging offence, and the "Red" magistrates were clearly prepared to launch Thomas and Moss in the direction of the gallows !

SWAN SONG FOR LAZENBY

While political violence was mainly confined to election times, there was always the normal, routine work to be attended to in between times, and Carmarthen's policemen—as illiterate and unreliable as ever—were now under the direction of an experienced officer and became more involved in tackling the town's disorderly drunks. It was a most daunting task because the "lower orders" had absolutely no respect for them, nor for the authority they represented, and every drunken prisoner had to be dragged struggling and fighting through the streets to the Cambrian Place lock-up, as often as not under the blows and epithets of a hostile mob.

The poor quality of the men under his command created many disciplinary problems for John Lazenby. His men were almost as drunken and unruly as anyone else in the town, and he seems to have done a good deal of the work himself. He was, for instance, to meet an old adversary again, in circumstances which showed that Carmarthen had merely returned from election riots to its "ordinary" level of violence, when—

"David Woolcock[3] was committed by the magistrates for two months to the treadwheel for attempting to burst open the Roundhouse door between 12 and 2 o'clock on Saturday morning, and for striking the Chief Constable while he was putting him in a cell in the Gaol, whither he was taken for want of room in the Roundhouse, *it being full of drunken men confined for fighting during the fair.*"[4] (C. J.)

David Woolcock, now a sailor, was a real rough handful in the town, and he made a number of appearances before the magistrates, as when they gave him six months for assaulting David Jones, a landlord of the Hare in Bridge Street, and when he was sent down for a month for violently assaulting two of the town's prostitutes, Jane Evans and Anne Perry, dislocating the arm of the latter.

He will return to the story early in 1836, in the most surprising circumstances.

Jane Evans, Anne Perry and other women of their kind—variously referred to as "common women of the town", "the frail sisterhood", and "nymphs of the pave"—did a roaring trade among the foreign sailors, and it was among the "frail sisterhood" that Constable David Rees demonstrated that Lazenby's policemen were not averse to making a shilling or two on the side, when he was—

" . . . suspended from his situation on a charge of the Chief Constable, under the following circumstances. It appears that a common woman of the town named Burnet, otherwise 'Betsy Cow', being pregnant, deputed Constable Rees to call upon an individual to say that if he did not send her some money she would swear her bastard with which she was pregnant to him. Under these circumstances he was induced to give Rees a Sovereign, fifteen shillings of which he gave to the girl and five of which he retained for himself." (C. J.)

It speaks volumes for the character of the police force in those days that Constable David Rees survived that affair and continued to serve for another two years, until, with his fellow

43

tearaway, Constable John Lewis,[5] he came to grief on the occasion of Carmarthen's annual free-for-all, Charter Day, and got the sack . . . for joining in on the wrong side in the traditional riot !

The consistently poor quality and unreliability of the constables meant that John Lazenby shouldered much of the peacekeeping burden himself, and contemporary accounts show that he was always in the forefront of the battle. He paid the price for his zeal one night in January, 1834, when—

> "A most atrocious attack was made upon Mr. Lazenby, Chief Constable of this town. A gang of eight ruffians, who have for some time past created riots and disturbances in our town, and many of whom were brought to justice on various occasions through the activity of Mr. Lazenby, determined to wreak their vengeance upon this active officer.
>
> On the night in question they assembled and concocted a plan to go to the street where he resides and there to get up a sham fight and cry out ' Murder ', which was accordingly done. Mr. Lazenby, on hearing the alarm, immediately rushed out to the crowd, and he was immediately surrounded by the villains, thrown to the ground, and trampled upon in a most violent manner. Had it not been for the assistance of some of the neighbours, he must inevitably have succumbed to the cowardly and diabolical attacks of these despicable wretches. The villains have absconded, but we trust sincerely that ere long they will meet with that punishment they so richly deserve." (C.J.)

Whether the "villains" were caught, and what happened to them if they were, remains a mystery, but, though no names were given in this account, we can safely bet that David Woolcock, John Woods and others of the 1831 election mob were not far away, for memories of 1831 were to dog poor Lazenby to the end.

John Lazenby's luck was indeed running out, because, though he could not know it, an event of September, 1833, foreshadowed the end of his career as a policeman. The tenor of the newspaper report of that event suggests that its significance also escaped the notice of others who would be affected by its consequences.

The *Carmarthen Journal* announced on Friday the 27th of September, 1833, that—

> "The Commissioners, Messrs. Austin and Booth,[6] investigating the state of the Corporations in South Wales, are to be at Carmarthen on Monday next from Brecon. In consequence of the disgraceful outrages which took place in this town on Charter Day (3rd of October, 1832[7]) they are, we understand, to be present at the appointment of the corporation officers and to report the proceedings of the day to government. This, we hope, will act as a check, and prevent the renewal of those outrages and disgusting scenes which were afterwards attended with so heavy an expense to the inhabitants at large. The leaders of the ' Mob ' have had, we hope, wisdom by experience and found that there is neither fame nor credit to be got by instigating drunken wretches to commit depredations on the property of their harmless and inoffensive neighbours." (C.J.)

Not a word of apprehension that those in power in the corporation might be found wanting. Not a word in the pro-corporation *Journal* to suggest that anyone but the opposition and its supporting "Mob" might be under scrutiny.

THE RECKONING

The bombshell fell in September, 1834, when the Commissioners presented their report,[8] of which no less than fifteen pages were devoted to a detailed examination of the government of Carmarthen—one of the two most corrupt boroughs in the kingdom !

The corporation stood condemned of flouting King George III's Charter by keeping the key decision-making in the hands of as few as *Eleven* burgesses, who favoured only their own adherents. It was further condemned of electoral fraud, includ-

45

ing the wholesale forgery of qualifications for election to the roll of burgesses ; of running up massive debts and virtually bankrupting the borough ; of the fraudulent disposal of landed property ; of rigging juries for the criminal courts by packing them with party men ; and of covering up their fiscal misconduct by failing to keep proper books of account for the previous forty years !

The Commissioners described how the ruling clique (and both "Red" and "Blue" were tarred with the same brush) packed the ranks of the voting burgesses with their tenants and friends, often from far-flung corners of the Kingdom, to give themselves a controlling majority. They found that—

> "For this purpose it has been usual to provide the person intended to be made a burgess with a fictitious property qualification within the borough. A formal conveyance of property to the requisite amount is prepared, but no consideration (money) passes, and no other act whatever is done. In this way, twenty or thirty persons have been made burgesses at the same time, *upon conveyance of a single mill, house or farm*. As soon as the admission takes place the conveyance is cancelled, and the property is conveyed again to another batch of fictitious owners. Instances were mentioned of a house or field having produced sixteen or twenty burgesses every three years."

Carmarthen democracy !

Party politics even intruded into the conduct of the lower civil and criminal courts for which the corporation was responsible under its Charters. The Commissioners found that there was a—

> " . . . political bias under which the judges, jurors and officers of the court are known to act in the ordinary business of the corporation and believed by their opponents to act in the discharge of their judicial duties. With respect to the judges and officers of the court, they are all (except the deputy recorder) elected by the burgesses for reasons (their political partiality) already described."

The corporation was supposed to have no control over the conduct of the Assizes, for His Majesty's Judges were men of the highest integrity. But the dispensation of justice depended even more on the integrity of their jurymen. Consider, then, the state of affairs arising from the fact that—

> "owing . . . to the political character of the officers who select and summon the juries, as well as of the jurymen themselves, the majority of the jury is usually composed of partisans of the same colour. Hence it happens that verdicts both in the civil and criminal courts are frequently given from party bias, against justice and the merits of the case."

So much for Carmarthen justice !

Moving to the management of the borough gaol, the Commissioners tersely noted that—

> "The present gaoler is a burgess of the corporation party. His predecessor was a burgess of the opposite colour, who was turned out when the present party came into power."

As to the state of Carmarthen's "Police force" :

> "The Police force consists of a chief and twelve petty constables. Of the present constables, three are small tradesmen and the rest belong to the labouring class, some of whom are not householders. They are described by the best authority as "very ineffective", *only four of the whole number being active officers.*
>
> The chief constable, though nominally at their head, has no means of exercising an effective control or compelling obedience to his directions.[9]
>
> With respect to the mode of appointment, it appeared that a servant of the corporation was lately dismissed from the office of constable ' *because he voted against the corporation,*' *and was succeeded by a burgess ' who voted for them.*'
>
> The intelligent chief constable suggested that the only means of obviating the evil was . . . by placing

47

(the force) under the direction of a commiss.oner un-
connected with either of the parties who contest the
rule of the corporation."

Thus did Carmarthen lead the Kingdom in municipal graft,
corruption and mismanagement, and thus did Carmarthen
earn its place in local government and police history with the
passing of the Municipal Corporations Act of 1835, which was
the inevitable consquence of this scathing report.

Reform and Revenge

The new act brought about a revolution in the government
of towns and in the representation of their inhabitants. The
ancient Royal Charters of some two hundred boroughs were
swept away. Their assets were in future to be applied for the
benefit of all. The extended voting rights given for parliamentary elections by the 1832 Reform Act would apply to borough
elections. Councillors would be elected by burgesses who held
that title as of right, basically through being rate-payers.
Burgesses could no longer become so by "gift or purchase"
and the burgess lists would be independently examined and
revised. The power of the council to sell and lease corporation
property would be severely curtailed and, in certain circumstances, made subject to the consent of His Majesty's Treasury.
Tight accounting and audit procedures would avoid the kind
of chaos found in Carmarthen by the Commissioners.

No longer would the appointment of magistrates be at the
whim of the local political majority ; they would be appointed
by the Crown through the Lord Chancellor, thus removing
political bias from the lower courts.

The "Watch" would be abolished and a new force of policemen, on the model of London's new Metropolitan Police, would
be recruited by a Watch Committee consisting of the mayor
and councillors. Most important of all, quarterly reports on
the force would be submitted to the Home Office in London.

Carmarthen's long-suffering people were about to enter a
Brave New World of Law and Order. Or were they ?

NOTES

[1]The Star and Garter, long since gone, stood about opposite the present Elephant and Castle, a few yards west of Saint Peter's Church.

[2]Author's Italics.

[3]One of the "Blue Seventeen" rioters of 1831.

[4]The Fairs, held in Carmarthen's narrow streets, regularly produced their crops of drunken prisoners.

[5]Under the alias "John my Maid", Lewis was convicted by the magistrates o violence several times over the next twenty years.

[6]Investigators for the Parliamentary Commission.

[7]The occasion of the attack on the Star and Garter.

[8]National Library of Wales.

[9]As in Tombstone and Dodge City, the Mayor was boss!

CHAPTER FOUR

A FORCE IS BORN

CARMARTHEN's first democratic borough council elections took place on the 26th of December, 1835. On the wave of an expanded electorate, the Whig radicals (the "Blues") swept into power, still rowdily supported by their "Mob", and the "Red"-controlled charter corporation was removed from office.

On the 1st of January, 1836, Carmarthen entered a new era of municipal government, and amid the general flurry of reorganisation its new civic leaders set about creating the "new" police force called for by the Act of Parliament. A mere nine months later, this letter appeared in the *Carmarthen Journal*, over the nom-de-plume "A Respectable Inhabitant" :

> "Sir ;
> We hope our townsmen are pleased with the new regulations of our municipal governors.
> The police force is now composed of persons who, to say the least, do but give authority to the old adage 'Set a thief to catch a thief'. Riotous and disorderly conduct among them is of so frequent occurrence as to call forth even the indignation of the magistrates themselves. This is in character. What more could be expected from men who have been dreaded by every peaceable inhabitant of the town ?
> Here, peaceable tradesmen of Carmarthen, are the men who are to defend your lives and property against the midnight attacks of robber and murderer. These are the men to whom is committed the preservation of the peace of the town. What mockery is this ?
> But the day of retribution will come, and these men, daring and reckless as they are, shall answer to their insulted townsmen for their conduct : Yours &c." (C.J.)

If our "Respectable Inhabitant" was to be believed, the

reality would seem to be falling somewhat short of the legislative dream. Well was it ?

After holding power for fourteen years by manipulating the burgess list, the "Reds" had been ousted by a party still smarting from the defeats of 1831 and 1832 and the imprisonment of its supporters. The result of the election had been a "triumph for the Whig radicals and a cause of exultation to the great unwashed".[1] And old habits would die hard in Carmarthen.

The new Watch Committee met for the first time on the 4th of January, 1836, under the chairmanship of the Mayor, the Whig war-horse Captain John George Philipps, and they immediately got rid of the man who had put Captain Philipps' followers in gaol in 1831 . . . Chief Constable John Lazenby. The minutes read thus :

> "Resolved that Mr. John Lazenby be discontinued in the office of chief constable for this borough, and that Mr. Joseph Morris (of Quay Street) be appointed to that office in his stead, *without any salary*, agreeably with his own proposal to this committee.
>
> It is further resolved that the following men be appointed assistant constables, viz—Richard Evans (Army Pensioner), The Parade ; Nicholas Martin (shoemaker), Lammas Street ; Charles Miller (shoemaker), King Street ; John Davies (hatter), Catherine Street ; Thomas Thomas (barber), Friars Court ; David Lewis (carpenter), Cambrian Place ; John Thomas (grocer), Lower Water Street ; Edmund Parry (labourer), Lammas Street."

Those few lines contain the whole message. The Chief Constable is to be a party man—a "Blue"-voting burgess with no other qualification for the job. The force is not to be paid a salary, but is to depend, as did the "Watch," on odd fees. For all but three or four of them the title "Constable" is to all intents and purposes an honorary one. Those who are "active" are as old and illiterate as their predecessors. And two of the new ones (Thomas Thomas and David Lewis) were among the imprisoned anti-"Red" rioters of 1831 . . . the "Blue Seventeen"!

Two days later the committee expressed its impatience at what seemed to be the reluctance of John Lazenby to relinquish his post. Directing that the Town Clerk give written notice for the handing over of "arms, accoutrements and other necessaries" provided for the use of the old police force, the Watch Committee threatened that—

> " . . . in the case of (his) neglecting or refusing to give up the same, that the said Joseph Morris (the new Chief Constable) is hereby empowered to take such proceedings as the Town Clerk shall advise for such refusal or neglect."

And the new town clerk was none other than Lazenby's old adversary, George Thomas, attorney, acquitted rioter, and the darling of the mob !

Here was crystallised the impossibility of changing attitudes or behaviour overnight (or even overyear !) by legislation. George Thomas, arrested by Lazenby just over three years before and charged by him with Riot, had turned the tables and was now to get his revenge. Lazenby, one of the founder members of the London Metropolitan Police, a professional policeman who had demonstrated an integrity uncommon in Carmarthen by telling the Parliamentary Commissioners that his force should be removed from political control, had paid the price.

John Lazenby was to leave Carmarthen and policework, to become Governor of Brecon Gaol.

If Lazenby kept in touch with happenings in Carmarthen after his dismissal, he must have smiled wryly to hear that within five months of it, George Thomas had gone the same way. On the 25th of May he was sacked by the council . . . . and took all the corporation books and accounts with him !

If any more evidence were needed to show that police and politics were still inextricably linked in Carmarthen, it came at a meeting of the Watch Committee on the 2nd of February, 1836, following another riot in the town when the Chief Constable and his Constables were paid three shillings and sixpence (17½p) each "for their diligence and exertion" in tackling the rioters. Was this another riot with political overtones ? Very likely.

52

The minutes go on to introduce more names last encountered in the trials following the 1831 election riots. The Committee resolved that—

> " . . . the sum of two shillings (10p) each be paid to John Rees, *David Woolcock, Thomas Thomas, John Woods* and David Howell, for their diligence and exertion in assisting the said Chief Constable when called upon by him in the performance of his duty."

What a coincidence that the very men who had been the ringleaders of the reform riots and spent time in Carmarthen's town gaol should be handy when needed by a police force led by one of the party in whose support they had rioted, and largely manned by their fellow rioters !

Three days later, a list of four extra constables appointed in view of " . . . the constabulary force being insufficient to preserve the peace of the town" contained the name of George Thomas, Quay Street, ship's carpenter . . . another of the "Blue Seventeen".

Quite clearly, the street war between "Red" and "Blue" was far from over.

The unsureness of the committee about its real aims is illustrated by the fact that no less than seven meetings were held between January and May, 1836, bringing about so many changes in the size and composition of the force, and so many changes of mind about how it should be employed, as to suggest that the new principles had not been fully grasped . . . if there was ever any intention to grasp them. In fact, they were back where they had started. It was the "Watch" all over again. But the Watch Committee did, at least, begin to have second thoughts about the fitness for office of its "Party man", Joseph Morris, the Chief Constable, because at a meeting on the 23rd of June the Mayor reported—

> " . . . that there was a most excellently recommended police officer at ye Municipal Police Office in London, who had offered to come as head officer here for £80 per annum."

That officer was being somewhat optimistic about the generosity of Carmarthen's council, because it was further ordered—

> " . . . that ye Mayor do communicate with him to know if he would take a less sum than £80 per annum"(!)

In that month, the committee at last set about clothing its policemen uniformly, in a manner befitting a "new" police force, in high-stocked tail coats of blue cloth with silver buttons, white "duck" trousers and black leather top hats, at a total cost of four guineas (£4.20p).

So, at last, Carmarthen had a body of men that looked like a police force—albeit basically a small one of only five men—but even by September, 1836, only nine months after the new Borough Police Force had been created, its character was clear. The new party in power had rewarded those who had led the mob in its support in 1831 and 1832—those violent men John Evans of the Ball Court, David Woolcock, George Thomas, John Thomas and Thomas Thomas were all being appointed constables.

No wonder our "Respectable Inhabitant" was moved to write to the Carmarthen Journal about the recruitment of "men who have been dreaded by every peaceable inhabitant of the town" !

The repercussions of such appointments as these would be felt in Carmarthen for a long time to come, but at least it can be said that the Watch Committee had discovered the measure of its "Party Man", Joseph Morris. They dismissed him in September, 1836, and appointed "ye most excellently recommended police officer from London" . . . . John Hall, who got his £80 per annum after all. Though he, a professional policeman, asked for six men, the committee allowed him only four. He was supported by a magistrate member of the committee, Edmund Hill Stacey, who had his protest entered in the minutes, pointing to the false economy sought by his opponents. Here was a town afflicted by nightly riots, while its elected rulers argued about the employment of two men—the difference between four and six policemen—at ten shillings (50p) each a week.

To be fair, though, Carmarthen was behaving no differently from the rest of the country, because the new police forces everywhere were up against this combination of tight-fistedness and hostility. Regular police forces were looked upon, even by the "upper classes", with the gravest suspicion as potential instruments of central government, and the "lower orders" had never had any respect for policemen of any kind. The new police of the cities and towns created by the 1835 Act were reviled and ill-used even by "respectable" people.

Chief Constable John Hall did not last long anyway. He had gone within a year, but a gap in the records leaves the unanswered question, why ? The fact that in November, 1837, a new Chief Constable, John Pugh, was appointed—at a salary of some £30 per annum less than Hall's—suggests that Hall had either resigned in disillusion or had been dismissed for expecting too much in the way of support or enthusiasm for a properly organised police force.

But hadn't Carmarthen seen off "London Policemen" before ?

From this point in November, 1837, it is worth glancing ahead two years, to note that the appointment of David Woolcock and John Woods (who was to become the Chief Constable's bitter and violent enemy) rounded off the employment at some time or other of every leading figure of the Reform Riots of 1831 !

Truly, the Whig Radicals had finally rewarded those of the "Great Unwashed" who had helped them to power.

THE MAYOR'S MAN

But the chickens of the 1831 riots would come home to roost on the heads of the Whig councillors who had tied themselves to violent men. The last and most blatant of these appointments backfired with a vengeance.

John Woods was a drunken thug, the most violent of the Reform rioters, and he would never have been entertained as a candidate for the police force by a properly constituted Watch Committee—even a Whig controlled Watch Committee—so his friend, Mayor David Morris, had him quietly sworn in before himself and two magistrate members of the committee after a court sitting one morning in January, 1840. Signifi-

55

cantly one of the other magistrates was Captain John George Philipps, the Whig candidate of 1831 in whose support the mob had rioted.

Challenging the manner of Wood's appointment, Alderman William Morris said—

> "As to the fact of there being three of the watch committee present, if that were allowed as a precedent, what was to prevent three of the watch committee from walking down the street and appointing anyone they might happen to meet ?" (C.J.)

What indeed ? Alderman Morris said that he and the other members of the committee knew nothing of Woods' appointment until they saw him walking around the streets in uniform on a Saturday morning !

In the face of the Mayor's support for Woods, the attempt to revoke the appointment failed, and he survived a stormy three months more, before even the Mayor had to acknowledge his outrageous behaviour. In April, 1840, Woods, by now thoroughly feared in the town, was before the Watch Committee for violence towards a "common woman of the town", Jane Evans, in a fracas in King Street, for which he was reprimanded. When Woods appeared before the committee on fresh charges, two weeks later, the case against him demonstrated both how far he had pushed Chief Constable Pugh towards resignation, and how the Mayor's protection was keeping Woods in the force :

> "Pugh reported P.C. Woods, first for having taken a person in charge and having let him go again without bringing him to the station house, secondly for bringing a false charge to the station house, and thirdly for being insolent to him (Pugh), being at the time in a state of inebriation." (C.J.)

The Chief Constable's evidence was corroborated by several townspeople and Alderman Morris said that Woods ought to be instantly dismissed :

> "The real question was whether Woods or Pugh was to be in charge. Pugh then said that sooner than put

The Committee at last set about clothing its policemen uniformly in a manner
befitting a "New Police Force"

up with a continuance of the insolence that Woods had lately given him, he would resign tomorrow.

The Mayor then said that he believed that Woods had erred in judgement; he moved that he be reprimanded.

Mr. Morris was quite certain that if they retained him, before a fortnight was over there would be another complaint against him. Woods was then called in and reprimanded by the Mayor *in a tone ' more in sorrow than in anger!* ' " (C. J.)

With as staunch a supporter as the Mayor, Woods would take some moving, but it obviously could not last, and Woods' short, violent career as a policeman ended in quite a dramatic fashion a month later at a meeting of the Watch Committee on the 26th of May, 1840, when—

"Chief Constable Pugh charged policeman John Woods with having been absent from his beat for upwards of three hours, and that when he found him he was in company with a prostitute ; that he was then drunk and extremely insolent, saying ' He did not care for Pugh any more than he did for the fifth wheel of a coach.' The Chief Constable likewise complained of Thomas Evans for having been off his beat in company with Woods, and of David Woolcock (another election rioter) for being off his beat." (C.J.)

With three quarters of his four-man police force charged before the Watch Committee, the hapless Chief Constable said that—

" . . . he merely brought the charge forward against Woods as a specimen of his general conduct ; that he was always either drunk or insolent, and that if he was to continue longer in the force, he (Pugh) would give up his situation.

Woods was then told that he was dismissed, and he then said "Am I to consider myself dismissed ?"

The Mayor : "You are."

Woods : "Mark me then, Pugh ; you are a deceitful, white-livered, treacherous coward. You have taken the bread out of my mouth, but if ever there is an election in this town again, your name will be ' Walker.' I have suffered five months solitary confinement for the party, and this is my reward. However, I got the party in and I will get them out. I am a freeholder, and at the next election you shall see how I will vote. As for you, Pugh, I do not care for you any more than I care for the fifth wheel of a coach. I am a better man than you are, so look to yourself."

After proceeding with such a torrent of genuine Billingsgate language as we never heard equalled, without interruption for nearly twenty minutes, he was kindly persuaded by the Mayor to withdraw.

Upon Pugh's attempt to leave the hall, Woods seized him by the collar and struck him a severe blow, for which he received one in return. The Mayor, who by a strange fatality has always protected Woods, stepped between them and prevented any further affray.

We understand that Pugh will not bring a charge against Woods for assault if he behaves himself for the future." (C.J.)

To Sign the Pledge ?

Having got that thorn out of its Chief Constable's side, the Watch Committee (over-optimistically, as it turned out) set out to improve the quality of its police recruits by deciding that—

"No person should be appointed to the office of constable without a written character from two respectable householders for sobriety and general good conduct.

Mr. Alfred Thomas suggested that in consequence of the many complaints of drunkenness against the policemen, *none should be appointed unless he had previously signed the teetotal pledge.*"[2] (C.J.)

Mr. Alfred Thomas' suggestion was not taken up, but even the resolution turned out to be mere wishful thinking; the drink problem would dog the force for many more years yet. In its first five years, for example, the force of four constables lost at least twelve men (and probably many more) through dismissal for drunkenness. John Evans (the younger) lasted for two months, and his brother, rioter John Evans of the Ball Court, a further seven. William Thomas of Red Street survived for six weeks before being found "drunk and incapable" on the pavement of his beat, as were William Williams and Robert Richards, after eighteen months and three years respectively. Those who survived for as long as Williams and Richards made many appearances on charges of drunkenness before the Watch Committee's patience ran out.

Likeable, illiterate Irishman, Nicholas Martin, demonstrated the indestructibility that would see him through twenty-five harum-scarum years, during which he survived at least forty-four disciplinary convictions. A founder-member of the force in January, 1836, he was to prove a steadfast, though evidently undisciplined, officer through to 1861, a period which saw the evolution of the force from a rowdy band of drunkards to something nearer to our conception of a police force. It was a period during which he outlasted six chief constables and saw the army draw its sabres for the last time in support of Carmarthen's policemen.

It did not take him long to win the respect of a substantial enough body of people in the town, because when he was dismissed on the 27th of December, 1839, for drunkenness, he was reinstated only four days later " . . . on the petition of numerous ratepayers."[3] His first recorded conviction before the Watch Committee, in January, 1838, brought a reprimand for " . . . being found tippling and off duty at the ' Marquis of Granby' public house,[4] at a quarter to two o'clock on Sunday morning the 21st of January."

The frequency of such disciplinary charges caused the Watch Committee, on the 23rd of June, 1840, to resolve that—

" . . . in future any police constable reported as having been in a public house or off his beat, being sober be fined two shillings (10 pence), to be deducted from his week's pay, and if drunk to be dismissed, and that the Chief Constable be directed to apprise his men of the determination of the Committee."

But time would tell. The Watch Committee's "Discipline" record book covering the next thirty years or so gives ample evidence of the futility of expecting too much in the way of sobriety among Carmarthen's early policemen, drawn as they were from the "lower orders", among whom drunkenness was endemic. Drunk or sober, though, they did their physically demanding job well in an age when the drunk and the violent had respect (albeit a grudging respect) only for the man who could, single-handed, propel him through a hostile and violent crowd to the lock-up.

Running the gauntlet in this way was to be the constables' lot in Carmarthen for many years, even to within living memory, and a very typical example of it came before magistrates William Phillips (the Mayor), Thomas Morris and William Rees Davies, at the Guildhall in March, 1839, when—

> "John James, alias ' John Bull', was brought in custody from the station house charged with being a party in a most brutal assault on Jones, the police constable, early on Sunday morning last. The evidence adduced before the magistrates went to show that Mr. Bull being at three o'clock on the morning in question drunk and creating a disturbance in the public streets, was taken into custody by Jones and Richards, aided by Pugh, the Chief Constable. Removing the prisoner to the station house, the police officers were surrounded by a gang of ruffians, who overpowered and abused them in a most cruel and heartless manner. Pugh was much abused and brutally kicked on the head while on the ground, by which he was completely stupefied. The case was clearly proved against Master Johnny, who was committed to the tread-wheel for two months.
>
> The other ruffians have decamped, but the police are in hot pursuit and the magistrates are determined to make an example of them." (C. J.)

We are all products of our time, and Carmarthen's early policemen were no less so, but whatever their frailties, they ran the gauntlet and they may lay a just claim to a good deal of the credit for the taming of this Wild Western town.

HIGH SPIRITS AND WOODEN HORSES

Even aside from its violence, the Carmarthen of the 1830s and the 1840s was as lively a little town as ever, for there was a different kind of boisterousness in the townspeople, of all classes, that awaited only the spark of a visiting circus, a river regatta, a horse-race meeting, a fair or any such open-air event for it to explode onto the streets in colour, music and movement in the full flourish of Carmarthen's special brand of high spirits.

Christmas Eve provided such a spark. It was another traditionally lively occasion, something of a climax in Carmarthen's boisterousness. It had many of the characteristics of the American Wild West, as crowds of all classes of people drank, sang and fought, to a backdrop of crackling fireworks and galloping, pistol-firing horsemen. Christmas Eve in Carmarthen is an experience not to be missed even in the 1980s, but it is not a patch on those of the mid-nineteenth century. A typical account of what was known as "Torch Night" described how, in the "principal streets of the town, particularly Guildhall Square", crowds of men and boys carrying flaming torches threw crackers squibs, fireworks and burning turpentine balls, and rolled blazing tar barrels. Girls and women found themselves the principal targets for squibs and crackers in a long night of wild and noisy excitement.

Another lively custom is mentioned in a report of December, 1837, in which it was coupled with the then familiar, and no doubt justified, taunt of political bias on the part of Carmarthen's police :

> "We heard that all the parties convicted of disorderly practices this (Christmas) week were men of Conservative (Red) opinions. If this be true, it would seem that the vigilance of the police is one-sided, for after the

61

exhibition of an *effigy* and its attendant disturbance, they could not lack opportunities for exhibiting their anxiety of preserving the peace by bringing up a few of the other side." (C.J.)

The "Effigy" was a "Ceffyl Pren", or wooden horse, which in older times had been a wooden frame on which an adulterer was bound and carried in procession through the town, to be pelted wth missiles such as rotten vegetables as a punishment for his or her sin. The mid-nineteenth century version of the "Ceffyl Pren" was a sort of Guy Fawkes—a straw filled effigy of the adulterer (or even a political opponent !)—which at the end of its tour through the town was burned on a bonfire, to the delight and noisy excitement of the large following. It could be the next thing to a riot, which was often the final outcome.

We shall hear more of the "Ceffyl Pren", through to the end of the nineteenth century, particularly during the Rebecca Riots, when it formed the basis not only for the destruction of the toll-gates, but also for the nocturnal "righting" of other social "evils" through, for example, the forcible reconciliation of husbands and wives. It was also a way of "persuading" young men to marry girls who were pregnant by them, of enforcing the support of bastard children (of whom there were large numbers) and of subduing wife-batterers, in all of which proceedings the "lower orders" would join with relish.

DISTANT THUNDER

As the eighteen thirties drew to their close, the people of Carmarthen might have taken a passing interest in the report of a disturbance at a small country cross-roads some twenty-five miles west of their town.

Having enough violence of their own to occupy their thoughts, it is unlikely that most of them attached much importance to the incident. They could not know that a fuse was being lit that would eventually cause a bigger than average bang in

62

Carmarthen, with a blast that would blow its Chief Constable right out of a job !

Under the heading "Serious Riots," the *Carmarthen Journal* reported that—

"About a fortnight since, in the night, a mob set fire and destroyed nearly the whole of the toll house at a place called *Efeilwen*, near Llandisilio, in the County of Pembroke.

About half past ten o'clock on the evening expected (an informant had warned the magistrates), a mob of about four hundred men dressed in women's clothes, and others with their faces blackened, marched to the toll gate huzzahing for free laws and toll gates free to coal pits and lime kilns, and after driving the constables from their stations and pursuing them to the fields adjoining, they returned to the gate and most outrageously set to work in demolishing the toll gate and toll house, and within the course of three hours the house was torn down to within three feet of the ground, the gate shattered to pieces with large sledgehammers, and the posts of the gate sawed off and carried away.

On Saturday night last, a third riotous mob marched on, armed with guns &c, to a toll gate near Saint Clears, Carmarthenshire, and after firing off several guns set to work to destroy the said gate &c, and in a short time there was hardly a vestige of either toll gate or toll house to be seen." (C.J.)

Thus was reported in Carmarthen the first skirmish in Rebecca's war on the toll gates, a campaign which would reach its violent climax four years later.

NOTES

[1] *Carmarthen Journal.*
[2] Author's Italics.
[3] Watch Committee minutes.
[4] Still open for business at the corner of King Street and Little Water Street.

CHAPTER FIVE

BECA

WRITING to the Home Secretary in June, 1843, at the height of the Rebecca riots, a Carmarthenshire attorney warned:

> "If Her Majesty's Ministers think there is nothing more in these disturbances than a mere local impatience of Turnpike Tolls, they are deceived."[1]

Edward Charles Lloyd Hall was close enough to the country people to perceive that as with Reform, so it was with the toll gates ; Rebeccaism was another label to which the struggling farmers, the poor country people and the labouring poor of the towns could pin their many grievances. He summarised the true and sorry nature of the troubles with a rare insight, cautioning those in London that—

> "To judge of ye Welsh and their feelings and modes of thought and action by anything with which an Englishman is acquainted would only lead to error.
> That they have had great local injustice in many things is too apparent, and unfortunately there is no middle class in ye country districts to bind society together. The few gentlemen resident here are widely scattered, their homes being in but few instances less than four miles from each other. The consequence is that each amongst his own tenantry is a petty prince, whose word, be it right or be it wrong, has hitherto been law ; and there being hardly any distinction between ye farmers and their labourers, and their language isolating them from ye rest of ye Kingdom, they have scarcely emerged from ye state of comparative barbarism and poverty induced by ye internal troubles of this part of ye country.
> This being ye case, and ye unfortunate measures of ye Government having fallen upon us with a severity

unknown to ye rest of England, ye farmers are pinched in their means, and as Turnpike tolls are most extraordinarily heavy, and ye gates placed upon ye most catching system throughout this country, they naturally endeavour to relieve themselves of that burden. There being a custom in this part of ye country called carrying "Ceffil prens"[2] (derived from ye old Welsh law abolished by ye introduction of ye English law in ye latter part of ye reign of Henry ye 8th) ye mode of getting rid of such a grievance by nocturnal violence is perfectly familiar to their minds.

As to getting evidence against them, that is hopeless. In ye best of times it is difficult to make a Welshman speak ye truth, either with or without an oath, no doubt attributable to ye curious provisions of ye old Welsh laws, traditionary reminiscences of which still remain. The offer of a reward, however great, has I believe never been known to produce any effect in this country.

If this state of things is not repressed very shortly, ye efforts of Rebecca will, I have no doubt, be directed to other matters ; for ye dissatisfaction with ye mode of administering justice and ye laying on of taxation of all kinds is such, throughout ye whole of this part of ye country, that it is quite palpable they only want leaders to effect a thorough revolution.

The people have thus discovered their immense power without knowing how to use it constitutionally.[3]

The remedy for this state of things cannot be a sudden one. Ye people must be made to feel, I believe, that justice is done them with a perfectly *even hand*. I have no hesitation in saying that such is not their feeling at present, and I am sorry to say that I can in several instances confirm ye fact that they have been right in their notion.[4] There are also several Acts of Parliament which press peculiarly hard in Wales."[5]

Times were indeed hard. Agriculture was depressed, labourers' wages were low, rents were high and they and the hated tithes[6] bit deeply into the pockets of people who were hard pressed to earn enough for food. It has been calculated that the net income of many small farmers was hardly different from that of labourers (hence the writer's reference to the lack of distinction between them), and that they were thus on a downward spiral towards destitution. One can imagine, therefore, the sense of grievance felt by a farmer making several journeys a day with his horse and cart to fetch lime for his fields, and having to pass through and pay toll at half a dozen gates.

Another hated institution, another symbol of oppression, was the Union Workhouse. It, too, came under attack during the Rebecca period, although as a secondary target, almost as an afterthought.

Carmarthen's workhouse on Penlan Hill was administered by the Carmarthen Union, a grouping of parishes brought about by the Poor Law Act of 1834 to improve the administration of the "Poor Rate". The system which the unions had replaced had become an expensive shambles under the strain imposed by the tremendous social changes of the late eighteenth and early nineteenth centuries. Things had reached the state where able-bodied men and their families were thrown onto parish relief by unemployment in such numbers as to swamp a system designed only to provide for the sick and the aged. A century of land enclosures had deprived many country people of the subsistence they derived from free grazing and driven them to the towns or onto parish relief.

How could the parishes be relieved of the able-bodied poor ? Simply, so the theory of the new poor law said, by ending their parish relief and giving relief to them and their families only in the workhouse, where they would repay it in honest toil. As a deterrent to poverty it was effective ; husband and wife were separated within the workhouse, tobacco and alcohol were banned, the diet was sufficient but basic, the regime prison-like, and the "honest toil" for the able-bodied consisted of breaking stones . . . a daily quota of fifteen bushels, or about one and a half tons !

None but the most desperate would seek relief within the walls of the workhouses, which soon acquired all the infamy

66

of the Bastille. A *Carmarthen Journal* report of the 24th of May, 1844, shows how the magistrates courts backed the system:

> " . . . before E. H. Stacey Esquire, and Captain J. G. Philipps (magistrates)—John Brian, Charles Hooper, John Jones, Thomas Canby, Sidney Smith and John Phelps were committed to the House of Correction yesterday for refusing to break the usual quantity of stones. They are all vagrants and one of them, Sidney Smith, appears by his dress to have *made his escape* lately from a Union Workhouse in the County of Somerset." (C. J.)

That such cases were common is shown by a comment in the *Carmarthen Journal* under the heading "Refractory Paupers" that—

> "The germs of incipient rebellion and treason on a small scale would appear to lurk in the workhouse of the Carmarthen Union. Since the (Christmas) holidays, when the inmates rejoiced in the ' seasonable liberalities ' which the press (not the paupers !) boast of everywhere, there has been nothing but risings and mutinies against the stonebreaking. Within the last week about half a dozen paupers were committed to prison for refusing to break them."

If the workhouse had a particularly severe "Master",[7] not even ill-health would procure exemption. It was no wonder that people looked up towards the gaunt, grey edifice on Penlan Hill with a cold shiver.[8]

WATER STREET GATE

For four years since Efailwen there had been sporadic attacks on toll gates (indeed, such attacks had occurred as far back as 1735), but it was the year 1843 that saw the most sustained violence, as the disguised and face-blackened mobs, armed with all manner of weapons and each with its female-garbed "Rebecca" at its head, descended on the toll gates in the dead of night to burn the toll houses and smash the gates. Private grudges were vented in the burning of hayricks and the destruction of country properties. Solidarity and numbers were maintained by the terrorising of country people into joining Rebecca's procession.

The "respectable" inhabitants of Carmarthen anxiously watched Rebecca's flame scorch the countryside, ever closer, knowing that it could only be a matter of time before it would lick at the town's own gate in Water Street. What they could not have foreseen, though, was the rare brazenness displayed by the Rebeccaites in the strength and the manner of their invasion of the town.

The Water Street Gate lay across the road to Trevaughan and Cynwyl Elfed, a hundred and eighty yards from Saint Catherine's Street, and the toll house stood by the Morgan's Arms public house.[9] It was a particular irritant to the country people because they felt it should have been made redundant by the opening of the new turnpike road to Cardigan through Glangwili. It could not, of course, because its removal would have encouraged travellers to abandon the new road in favour of the old.

Henry Thomas, the keeper of the Water Street Gate,[10] slept in his clothes because he was liable to be called out to open the gate at any hour of the night. There was a knock on his door at ten minutes to one o'clock on the morning of Saturday the 27th of May, 1843 . . . it was a man with a cart returning late to town. The toll was taken, the gates closed again, and Henry Thomas returned to his little toll house, where his wife and child were sleeping, and settled down again on his bed with every hope that he would not be disturbed again that night.

The sound seemed to rush on him suddenly—a "thundering noise" outside—and there could be no doubt of what was happening. The "celebrated Welsh Outlaw, Rebecca, and her ' sister ' Charlotte and about three hundred of her children"[11] had come at last to Water Street Gate.

Henry Thomas was out of his bed like a shot and ran to the door, but—

" . . . before he could reach there, the door was struck in against him and Rebecca and her sister came into the passage. He saw it would be quite useless to make any resistance and said in order to save himself being ill-treated, ' Oh, Beca is here ; go on with your work, you are quite welcome.'

Rebecca desired him not to be alarmed, as they would do no injury whatever to him. The gatekeeper then begged them not to destroy the furniture as it was his own and that his wife and child were in bed, but they might do as they liked with the gate and tollhouse. Rebecca went to the door and ordered her daughters not to touch anything but the gate and the roof of the house, but not to break the ceiling for fear they would come onto the woman and child in bed.

In their hurry to unroof the house, one of them slipped between the rafters and his foot got through the ceiling, and Rebecca expressed sorrow at the accident, as it might cause some inconvenience to the gatekeeper. During the whole of that time, the work of destruction was carried out in a most furious manner, with large hat-chets and cross-saws, and a number of men had taken a ladder and ascended to the roof of the house, which was completely stripped in a very short time." (C.J.)

The crashing of the building and the roar of the mob carried across the still night air to Cambrian Place and the station house, from where John Pugh and his four policemen rushed to the bottom of Water Street . . . to be met by blasts of shot, for—

"Before they commenced breaking the gate, Rebecca had taken the precaution of placing about a dozen of her daughters with guns in their hands as sentinels to guard the street leading to the centre of the town. They kept firing incessantly down Water Street, so that it was impossible for any person to approach them at the gate.

Rebecca and her sister were dressed in long, loose, wide gowns, with women's caps or turbans on their heads

69

and their faces blackened, and they had large swords in their hands. Nearly the whole of the rest were also dressed in women's clothes and the greater part of them were armed with guns.

The people living near the place got up to their windows, but they were immediately ordered back and they could distinctly hear the shots whistling as they passed them." (C.J.)

Within the space of fifteen or twenty minutes the work was done :

"The gate was broken to pieces and the posts sawed off about fifteen inches from the ground, and the lamp and gas-pipe destroyed. All the windows of the toll-house were smashed, the toll board taken down and split, and Rebecca informed the gatekeeper that had it not been for his spirit towards them, the house would have been taken down.

After the work of demolition was completed, Rebecca called in the sentinels, and they all left together towards Fountain Hall, making the most strange noises imaginable, seemingly trying to imitate the squeeking of pigs, but when they came up to Green Hall they stopped and fired ten or a dozen shots." (C.J.)

Needless to say, there were no arrests, and the police maintained their respectful distance from the three hundred rioters, who marched back into the hills of Newchurch and Talog from whence they had come, their shouts and gunfire fading as the hills enfolded them.

Well, who were Rebecca and Charlotte that night ? The popular belief is that Rebecca was a young farmer named Michael Bowen of Trelech[12] ; indeed the Carmarthen historian Alcwyn Evans, then a boy of fifteen, claimed to have recognised him despite his black face and long, ringletted wig, during the mob's second invasion of the town three weeks later. Certainly Bowen was among those convicted at Carmarthen Assizes, but another account[13] written in the Parish of Newchurch—the heart of this particular Rebecca's country—tells another story. Claiming to have come at first hand from a participant in the raid, Gaffer Thomas of Green Park, who was still living when the account was written in 1910, it tells us that Rebecca and Charlotte were in fact two Rees brothers, from Rhydymarchog farm, just along the road from Newchurch village, whose family had moved there from Cardiganshire only two years before.

The Rees family had brought from Cardiganshire three long trumpets such as were used in the nineteenth century to call in the harvesters and it was said that the trumpets' blast brought people running from all directions, fearful of the consequences of failing to answer the call. It was with the trumpets, Gaffer Thomas said, that the two Rees brothers followed by their large masculine sister, led the three hundred to the demolition of the Water Street Gate.

AMBUSH

When daylight came and the extent of the damage to the gate could be seen, the magistrates met to decide what should be done. The police not unnaturally came under their lash, and—

> " . . . were severely reprimanded by the magistrates
> for their cowardice in not making an attempt to put a
> stop to the law-less proceedings and capture some of
> the gang." (C. J.)

There was no comment on the relative ranges and effectiveness of the policemen's horse-pistols and the Rebeccaites' dozen or so shotguns !

A temporary gate was placed across Water Street and a few days later the extent of the intimidation of the country people by Rebecca became clear when John Harries, a fifty year old miller from Talog Mill, Thomas Thomas, a Talog shopkeeper, and Samuel Brown of Brynmeini, refused to pay the toll. They were each fined forty shillings (£2) and eight shillings and sixpence (42½ pence) costs—well over a month's wages for a labourer—despite their claim that their lives and homes would have been endangered if they paid the tolls. Proof of this was contained in a poster pinned to the door of Bwlch Newydd Chapel. In Welsh, it warned the parishioners that—

" . . . the goods of all persons who will henceforth pay at Water Street Gate will be burned and their lives taken from them at a time when they will not think. BECA."

Under these threats, John Harries and the others understandably failed to pay their fines, and the magistrates issued the usual warrants for the seizure of personal effects in lieu of the money. Somewhat naively they sent four special constables on foot the seven miles to Talog to execute the warrants, but the party got no further than Blaen-y-Coed village where, at a blast from a horn (one of the Rees' harvester horns ?) they were surrounded by forty or fifty black-faced men wielding scythes, sticks and forks.

The expedition had failed, and the specials were forced to walk back to Carmarthen empty-handed.

The magistrates were now faced with the need to show the ascendancy of the law over what they saw as the next thing to insurrection. There must be a show of strength . . . and there was. A posse of forty men was organised, and the discredited police were to have the support of a few specials and twenty-eight of the elderly pensioners (army reservists) living in the town. They would be led through the lanes of Trevaughan and Newchurch to Talog by the road surveyor, David Evans,[14] sworn in as a special constable, and the expedition would be carried out on foot, with arms, under cover of darkness, to arrive at dawn.

They lost one of their number before they even started. Shortly after midnight, in the early hours of Monday the 12th of June, David Evans assembled his party at the Water Street Gate. Of the regular police he had Nicholas Martin, David Woolcock, Robert Awberry and David Woozley (the station-house keeper), but of Thomas Evans there was no sign. He sent David Woolcock to find him, which he did, cowering in a doorway in Lammas Street. A trembling Thomas Evans refused to budge, and as Woolcock told the Watch Committee later—

" . . . he told me not to be so foolish to go to Talog or we should be murdered. I then desired him to deliver up his Pistols, which he did. I did not see him afterwards. Evans told me he was unwell."[15]

Through the darkness, into the hills, marched the posse, the police with pistols primed and loaded ; up through Trevaughan, past the Plough and Harrow public house,[16] and into the steep, winding lanes of the hill country, away up to Harries' mill at Talog. At half past five, in broad daylight, they confronted John Harries, who offered no resistance to the seizure of £4 or so worth of his furniture. Loading the furniture onto handcarts, they went to the nearby shop of Thomas Thomas, to find that he had paid his fine on the previous Saturday in order to avoid trouble at his home and upset to his pregnant wife.

Their job done, the posse began their march back to Carmarthen, but they were no more than a quarter of a mile along the road from Talog when Thomas Thomas (who obviously knew something they did not) breathlessly caught up with them and pleaded with them, for their own safety, to leave Harries' goods behind as the fine would be paid. He was too late. The long trumpet sounded and, seemingly from nowhere, they were surrounded by Rebecca and four hundred of her children, a hundred of them with loaded guns. The police and pensioners were immediately—

" . . . completely overpowered and were rigidly searched and compelled to fire their pistols in the air[17] and then deliver them up to Beca and her family, who were all disguised in various dresses. The mob then desired the force to fall into a line, and Beca inspected them to see if D. Rees[18] and Thomas, constables, were with them, and when she was satisfied they were not she said had they been there their lives would certainly be taken away.

They were then ordered to march to Trawsmawr, the property of Captain Davies, who was the County Magistrate who had endorsed the distress warrants issued by the Town Magistrates,[19] and when they arrived there

73

they *commanded* the constables to break down the walls surrounding the house, which they did in order to save their lives, which they threatened to deprive them of if they did not at once comply.

When this act of destruction had been completed, they shook hands with the pensioners and told them to go to their homes and they would not be molested.

They were not so polite to the constables, to whom they manifested considerable animosity. We have been told that the pensioners were not armed. Had they been, the result would likely have been very different. The arms taken from the constables were returned by Beca before she parted company with them." (C.J)

The defeated and disconsolate party of law-enforcers shuffled off on the four mile walk back to Carmarthen, hastened by a parting volley, which showered them with gunshot. What were they to say ? They had failed to execute the magistrates' warrants, they had been disarmed and were lucky to have their weapons back, and they had demolished the walls around the home of a prominent county magistrate !

Only Constables Nicholas Martin, the tough Irishman, David Woolcock, the "Reform" rioter, and Robert Awberry, one of the force's leading drunkards, came out of the incident with any semblance of credit. Only they had shown any hint of resistance to the overpowering mob, and when the Watch Committee eventually held its inquest and identified its scapegoats, they were rewarded with a "small gratuity".

Constable Thomas Evans was sacked, of course, and not even the petition of a hundred and twenty-two of "the most respectable inhabitants of the town" could persuade the Watch Committee to reinstate him.

The fiasco brought ridicule from all sides, and the army pensioners felt obliged to defend themselves in a letter to the *Carmarthen Journal* :

"We, twenty-eight out-pensioners of Her Majesty's Royal Hospital, Chelsea, now resident at Carmarthen and its vicinity, present the following facts for information of the public as well as for the justice due to ourselves relative to an affair whereby our courage as veterans has been called in question.

The charge of cowardice preferred against us cannot be substantiated. We feel we do not deserve it. What service could be rendered by twenty-eight decrepit individuals with no other weapons of defence other than constables' batons against such an armed number of able-bodied, active and incensed rustics ?

We spent the prime of life in the service of our country, we fought hard against its foes, and bled in distant lands. The fact of our being pensioners corroborates this assertion and are we now at this stage of life (most of us upwards of sixty years of age) to be branded as cowards because we did not cause ourselves in an undefended state to be slaughtered ?

We trust that this will satisfy all generous minds, and any duty we owe to our Sovereign and our Country we will always perform to the utmost of our ability. *God save the Queen.*" (C.J.)

But there was worse to come, and the signs were all around. Edward C. Lloyd Hall, the Newcastle Emlyn attorney, had visitors at his home :

"On my return home this afternoon (15th June, 1843), I found a deputation of about twenty farmers, residing in six or seven different parishes in this neighbourhood, waiting to consult me on ye steps I should deem it most advisable for them and those whom they represented to pursue in consequence of a number of letters having been sent by or in ye name of ye organized band known as Rebecca and her daughters, commanding them to appear at Carmarthen on Monday next (19th June) with their servants and under-tenants, on pain of having their houses pulled down if they dare to absent themselves.

The men appeared quite terrified at ye threat, and with reason, as ' Rebecca ' is almost nightly at work pulling down ye Turnpike Houses, and one house belonging I believe to Mr. Saunders Davies, M.P., with all ye furniture was burnt to ye ground three or four nights ago in consequence of ye tenant having done something to give offence to Rebecca."[20]

By letter, public notice, pulpit announcement and horse-messenger, the farmers and the other country people in the parishes of Cynwyl, Abernant, Newchurch, Trelech and Cilrhedyn were summoned to meet at the Plough and Harrow, two miles from Carmarthen on the Cynwyl Elfed road, at eleven o'clock on the morning of Monday the 19th of June, in order to march on the town to demonstrate their power. As Mayor Edmund Hill Stacey warned the Home Office :

> "The lawless gang calling themselves ' Rebecca and her children ' continue nightly to break down the Turnpike Gates in this neighbourhood, and have within the last two or three days held meetings, most numerously attended, at which it was determined, for the purpose of intimidating the Magistrates by a display of physical strength and inducing them to return the fines which had been paid for refusing payment of toll at the Water Street Gate, to enter the town on Monday next at noon to the number of many thousands.
>
> I have no force at my disposal adequate to preserve the peace unless the (promised) Cavalry should arrive here tomorrow.
>
> The country in which the Military force will have to act is in many parts hilly and much covered with wood and with high fences, which would render it rather impracticable for Cavalry to act unless assisted by Infantry, and I beg leave most respectfully to submit to you the expediency of sending down immediately a company of Infantry as well, the parties whose illegal proceedings we have to suppress being very formidable from their armed number and extensive organisation."[21]

Strong forces of troops were already in Wales to put down the Rebecca riots, and a troop of the 4th Light Dragoons, under Major Parlby, had been despatched from Cardiff in response to the Mayor's report on the Water Street Gate and Talog incidents. The arrival of this cavalry troop in the town was to be a dramatic one, reminiscent of the best of the American western tradition of the besieged wagon train !

INVASION !

Monday came—a hot, sunny June day—and the country people gathered in their hundreds at the Plough and Harrow. Rebecca was there in a fantastic wig of long, golden ringlets, mounted on her large horse in the centre of some three hundred other horsemen. The horns blew their message across the fields and through the deep, narrow valleys, and the huge crowd of two thousand on foot was somehow collected into a kind of order behind the horsemen.

Rebecca's army set off for its invasion of Carmarthen town behind a band (of sorts), the whole behind a large banner proclaiming—

"Cyfiawnder a Charwyr Cyfiawnder ydym ni oll"
("Justice, and lovers of justice are we all")

The police, still without the troops for which the magistrates had been pleading for several days, were out early that morning, they and the special constables having been ordered by the Mayor to assemble at the Guildhall at eight o'clock. Chief Constable John Pugh was there with his whole force—Nicholas Martin, David Woolcock, Robert Awberry and David Woozley —but the magistrates' orders to them were to lie low and to allow the procession to pass through the town if no breach of the peace were occasioned.

The town magistrates were joined by a large number of their county colleagues, two of whom, Captain Evans of Pant-y-cendi, and J. Lloyd Davies of Blaendyffryn, actually went up the road beyond Trevaughan to meet Rebecca and her followers near the Plough and Harrow and make a last minute plea to them to think again. The sight of such a huge number must have appalled them, and they could not have been surprised that—

77

" . . . our efforts, although attended with some personal danger, were unavailing."[22]

Personal danger there was indeed, for J. Lloyd Davies' home was visited during that day by a horseman who threatened that his house would be fired that night !

On marched the huge procession, the band playing, the sun and the carnival atmosphere banishing the fear and intimidation which had brought them there. As they approached the town, watchers noted with some little apprehension that—

" . . . a great number of idlers from the town had come over in order to meet them and prevail upon them to advance to Carmarthen to show their strength." (C.J.)

The "Carmarthen Mob", led by the "Dan-y-Banc Fishermen"[23] was gathering once again.

In Carmarthen itself—

" . . . the shops were closed and business was completely suspended. The streets were thronged with thousands of spectators waiting anxiously to get some information of Rebecca and her proceedings." (C.J.)

The whole town, and not the least its police, held its breath as the sound of the band, the harvesting horns and two and a half thousand people grew louder from the direction of Trevaughan village. And then, at half past noon—

" . . . an immense throng of Rebeccaites were seen coming by Fountain Hall, and in a few minutes they entered the town through Water Street Gate.

The procession consisted of about four thousand (?) men on foot and nearly five hundred on horseback, but there were a great deal of women and young boys among them. There were certainly a few respectable men to be seen in the procession, whom we hope were *compelled* to attend.

The greater part of them were a motley group of the most mean and low vagabonds that we have ever seen in our lives. Several of the town blackguards had comfortably seated themselves behind the men on horse-

78

back, and others were seen leading the procession through the town.

When the procession arrived at the Guildhall, they gave three hearty cheers, which were lustily responded to by groups of spectators who by this time completely filled Guildhall Square, so that the Rebeccaites could hardly pass through.

The procession then turned to the right, through Red Street, and proceeded directly to the Union Workhouse." (C.J.)

People said later that threats had been made against the workhouse during the various happenings of the past weeks, but the unpreparedness of the town authorities for what came next suggests that this may have merely been the product of hindsight.

There were at least "a hundred idle townspeople" loitering about the workhouse before the procession arrived, and when it did the mob hammered on the stout wooden gates and demanded admittance, which the master, John Ray Evans, at first refused—

" . . . but when the master saw the door on the point of giving way he opened it as he knew it would be forced in less than a minute. Hundreds of rioters immediately entered the yard and soon found their way into the house by breaking every lock which impeded their progress.

Some of them laid hold of Mrs. Evans, the Matron, by the arms and pushed her against the wall and ordered her to deliver the keys of the house or she would be a dead woman, when the workhouse children screamed out in a most piteous manner ' Oh dear mistress ; don't kill our dear mistress.'

Several of the others attacked the master and wrenched two keys from his hand and one of them knocked him down. Some of them proceeded to the men's yard, ordered them out of the place and attempted to enter their bedroom, where they were resolutely opposed, and they succeeded in stopping the rioters entering their own bedroom.

They then ordered the children out of the place. When Mrs. Evans remonstrated with them and said 'Where do you expect the poor children to go, they have no homes in the world ?' they answered 'We'll find them a home' and all the children and women were turned out into the road, where a poor woman of this town was severely hurt.

Others of the rioters had proceeded direct upstairs into the children's bedroom, being led by a woman who had lately been discharged from the workhouse,[24] and immediately commenced throwing the beds, blankets and pillows out through the windows into the yard. In fact the whole place was now in their possession. They had forced their way into the boardroom and were dancing on top of the tables and beating them with their staffs in a furious manner." (C.J.)

The Bastille had been stormed and it was said that the whole place would have been fired or razed to the ground in a very short time, but for the "special intervention of Providence".

Yes, Providence intervened . . . in the shape of Her Majesty's 4th Light Dragoons.

"SLASH AWAY ; SLASH AWAY"

The Dragoons were passing through Pontarddulais at a walk, and as they ascended the hill from the village, a messenger from Carmarthen brought the news that the mob was marching on the town. At a signal from Major Parlby, the horsemen, helmets flashing in the sun and plumes streaming put their mounts to the gallop and made an incredible sixteen mile dash to Carmarthen, up and down the steep hills and valleys in between, crossing the town bridge at a furious pace. Up Castle Hill, into Spilman Street they galloped, pausing breathlessly at the Ivy Bush Inn[25] to learn from magistrate Thomas Charles Morris that the workhouse was under attack.

The excited magistrate mounted his own horse and led the charge through the town and up Penlan Hill, where the Dragoons drew their sabres and hurtled into the mass of people surrounding the workhouse and packing its yard. Thomas Morris, entering fully into the spirit of his unaccustomed role, was heard shouting "Slash away, slash away", as the cavalry crashed into the mob.

The rioters had the fright of their lives and—

" . . . when (they) perceived the Dragoons galloping up towards the workhouse with drawn swords a scene took place which we can compare to nothing but the flight of the French from the plains of Waterloo.[26] 'Save himself who can ' was the order of the day. Those who were on horseback immediately galloped away through different lanes, and those on foot cut their way through the hedges and gardens and over fields of corn towards the country, without once looking back to see what would be the fate of their friends inside.

Several hundred of those inside scrambled over the walls and succeeded in making their escape, but when the military came up they immediately surrounded the walls to cut off the retreat of the rioters, and the special constables and the police rushed in and overcame those inside.

The mob attempted to offer resistance at first, and some of the constables were rather severely handled, but through the great exertions of the special constables they were soon overpowered. Upwards of sixty were taken and placed in confinement in the hall of the Workhouse.

When the military first rushed on, several very serious accidents occurred. One man who, it is reported, had struck one of the Dragoons with a stone received a severe sword cut on his head. A young shopkeeper of this town fell and one of the horses trod upon his arm and he had a fractured arm above the wrist. Others sustained less important injuries." (C.J.)

The riot was over . . . and justice was administered swiftly :

"As soon as the prisoners had been secured and the confusion had ceased, the Mayor, with the Borough and

County Magistrates, held a meeting on the spot. They sat in the Workhouse schoolroom. The prisoners were brought before them and examined as to their intentions of coming to Carmarthen, but they all had the same account to give of themselves, viz. that their houses had been threatened to be burned and their lives to be taken away. Some of them said that those threats had been published before the Churches and Meeting Houses on the Sunday previous. One man said that a notice to that effect had been stuck up on the door of his Parish Church." (C.J.)

Among those arrested was John Harries of Talog Mill, who was remanded to prison with the rest. He was later charged with being the author of some of the threatening letters which had forced so many to join the march. He had visited County Magistrate David Davies at Trawsmawr two days before the invasion of Carmarthen and handed him a letter threatening the invasion if the fines and distrained goods were not returned by the town authorities before the Monday.

It would be several months before the trials proper took place at Carmarthen's Assizes, but the 4th Light Dragoons, by their spectacular intervention,[27] had taken all the steam out of the Talog-centred Rebeccaites. While other toll-gates in West Wales suffered destruction during the remaining months of 1843, Carmarthen town had seen the last of Rebecca, though the town continued to experience the reverberations of the troubles in the surrounding countryside, in the shape of the to-ing and fro-ing of the army and members of the London Metropolitan Police. The 4th Light Dragoons were joined in the town by the 73rd, 75th and 76th Regiments of Infantry, and the 13th Light Dragoons. Colonel Love, the District Commander, took over the Workhouse as a barracks and there was a great deal of military activity as attacks were made on Glangwili House and on the toll-gates at Croeslwyd, and at many places further afield. The County authorities also obtained the services of fifty London policemen, under Inspector Martin, and many of them were billetted in the town of Carmarthen.

By the time the Carmarthen rioters came to trial in the
following Spring, the government and the courts, undoubtedly
influenced by a sympathetic series of reports in the London
Times newspaper, had recognised the validity of the grievances
which had driven the people to such extremes. Except for
sentences of transportation passed on a tiny number of the most
violent ringleaders of riots in other parts of Carmarthenshire,
sentences were light. The Carmarthen and Talog riots resulted
in sentences of twelve months hard labour downwards, most
of the prisoners being discharged without any sentence at all.

A special Assize in the Guildhall in March, 1844, dealt with
the Carmarthen and Talog rioters and with others from elsewhere in the County. An atmosphere of leniency pervaded the
whole of the proceedings against those who had engaged in
the Talog ambush and the attack on the Workhouse, and even
the Attorney General (whose presence at Carmarthen as pro-
secutor testified to the importance attached by the government
to the trials) had a favourable word to say of those who had
fled the field when the cavalry charged :

> " ' Conscience makes cowards of us all ' he said ; ' A
> Welshman would never show such cowardice were he
> not conscious of being engaged in a bad cause.' " (Cam)

An almost embarrassing series of tributes to the good character of the defendants, not only from prosecution witnesses, but
even from some County Magistrates, helped to save them from
an uncomfortable voyage to the Antipodes !

John Harries went to hard labour for twelve months, and
the Judge gave eight months hard labour each to David Thomas, to Job Evans, a forty-eight year old farmer, and to three
of the "idlers of the town" who had gone out to join the march
—David Williams, a twenty-seven year old weaver, Isaac Charles, a nineteen year old tailor, and John Lewis, forty year old
Dan y Banc coracleman.[28] Eight months hard labour was also
handed down to those who ambushed the police and the army
pensioners at Talog, or at least the five who could be identified.

Hard Labour meant back-breaking, leg-wearying hours on

the treadwheel, but at least they were not bound for Australia. There can rarely have been such sighs of relief in Carmarthen's Assize Court prisoners' dock !

It took only three weeks for the wrath of the Watch Committee to descend on Chief Constable Pugh and his men. Pugh was sacked, but "the conduct of the other police officers was overlooked on the grounds of their not having an efficient person to lead and direct them".

Pugh had been conspicious by his absence from much of the rioting, and had been left behind in the march on Talog, but he was at least in action in the workhouse yard arresting a number of people pointed out to him by the magistrates. He was assaulted by several of the rioters, including David Thomas, a twenty year old farmer and member of Rebecca's "Band of music", who hammered Pugh with his bassoon !

None other than Constable Nicholas Martin was selected to act as Chief Constable during the interval before a successor was found. It was a fleeting moment of glory for this tough, amiable, illiterate, hard-drinking Irishman.

At a later meeting, a resolution of the Watch Committee reflected Rebecca's loss of interest in Carmarthen town after her severe beating by the cavalry. Deciding that the police had enough to do with the town's normal disorderly state, they put an end to their use in guarding turnpike gates from the 23rd of September, 1843. That meeting also recorded a quietly historic moment. The town had just seen the use of troops to quell a disturbance in its streets (a "normal" and not a Rebecca disturbance) and the magistrates spelled out their determination that peace-keeping was henceforth to remain the responsibility of its policemen, now under the command of a new Chief Constable.[29] The minutes record that they—

> " . . . had heard with much satisfaction that the calling out of the Military last Saturday night did not originate with the Mayor and Magistrates, and they have to express a hope that in future they will not be permitted to act without a requisition from the Authorities of the Borough."[30]

No such "requisitions" were ever made again.

NOTES

1Edward C. Lloyd Hall, attorney, Emlyn Cottage, Newcastle Emlyn: Pub. Record Office, File HQ 45/454.

2See Chapter 4, page 62.

3Author's Italics.

4As an attorney, the writer regularly defended country people in the courts.

5Pub. Record Office, file HO 45/454.

6A form of tax for the upkeep of churches and clergy, based on the average yield of land. They had recently been increased by five per cent.

7Henry Winchcombe for example was dismissed in 1846, the last straw in a long series of cruelties being his refusal to admit a 3-week old child found abandoned in Little Bridge Street. He told the woman finder to "Leave the child where she found it."

8The building is still there.

9Still open for business in 1980.

10Henry Thomas was appointed to the Carmarthen Borough Police Force as a constable three years later.

11*Carmarthen Journal.*

12*The Rebecca Riots* (David Williams: University of Wales Press).

13"The History and Antiquities of the Parish of Newchurch", Carmarthenshire (The Rev. T. M. Morgan, Vicar, 1910).

14In preference to the disgraced Chief Constable, John Pugh, whose very future as Chief Constable was now at stake.

15Watch Committee minutes.

16Still open for business in 1980, two miles out of Carmarthen.

17They were single-shot muzzle loaders, which took some time to load; revolvers had not yet been invented.

18David Rees was a "Parish Constable" who was known to be infiltrating the Rebeccaites and informing on them to collect the rewards then on offer. He also obtained rewards from the Special Commissioners who were appointed later to investigate the Rebecca outrages, by giving evidence against the Rebeccaites, who had every reason to hate him. He died 30 years later at his home in Mill Dam Street, Carmarthen, at the age of eighty-two.

19To give them legal effect outside the Borough boundary.

20Letter to Home Secretary, 15th June, 1843; Pub. Record Office, File HO 45/454.

21Letter to the Home Secretary, Saturday 17th June, 1843; Pub. Record Office, File HO 45/464.

22Letter to the Home Secretary, Monday 19th June, 1843; Pub Record Office, File HO 45/454.

23Alcwyn Evans (Nat. Lib. of Wales Ms. 12368 E)

24Frances Adams, of Cilgwyn Uchaf, in the Parish of Newchurch.

25Still open for business in 1980.

26A nice historical touch is added to this event in the fact that the Dragoons drew their sabres and went into the charge as they turned into . . . Waterloo Terrace! The 4th Light Dragoons, including some of the veterans of Penlan Hill, would eleven years later charge with the Light Brigade at Balaclava.

27Two of their horses dropped dead of exhaustion, having covered sixteen miles in an hour and ten minutes under a scorching sun.

28The Lewis family must be one of the oldest in Carmarthen, having plied the river in their coracles for centuries, even to this day. Other families who feature in this story—the Thomases, the Eliases, the Evanses and others—are still with us.

29Henry Westlake (see next Chapter).

30Watch Committe Minutes.

CHAPTER SIX

CHIEFS AND DRUNKS AND NYMPHS

HENRY Westlake became Chief Constable of Carmarthen in August, 1843, at a salary of £80 a year (or £1.53 a week). He lasted for only nine months and his most notable feat was to be the cause of a riot in the town !

On the evening of September the 16th, new broom Henry Westlake decided to take a firm hand with Carmarthen's Saturday night revellers and fighting drunks. But he obviously underrated the "Carmarthen Mob". There was pandemonium. The town centre was a mass of flying fists, sticks and boots, with Westlake and his four constables getting very much the worst of it, when suddenly the cavalry arrived, clattering out of Red Street and scattering the crowd to all corners of the square.

The 4th Light Dragoons had done it again !

Who called them no one knew, but a much relieved Henry Westlake trod just that little more carefully in future, until he spied his chance to get out. His next job—as Governor of Carmarthen's County Gaol in succession to John Burnhill—no doubt gave him ample scope for the undisputed exercise of his "officious" manner.[1]

Henry Westlake's successor as Chief Constable—Edwin Young—came from the Cardiff force in answer to the corporation's advertisement. He served for three years and the reason for his leaving is not recorded, but nothing more than "routine" disorder seems to have occurred during his tenure of office.

TROUBLE IN THE RANKS

James Hill George succeeded Edwin Young. Another ex-Cardiff man, he had served in Carmarthen since September, 1843, and had been promoted Sergeant only one month after

86

his arrival in the Borough. But James Hill George was to prove something of a handful before he resigned just over a year after his elevation to Chief Constable. Within a month of his elevation , the Watch Committee was complaining about the number of cases of drunkenness in the ranks, and disciplinary convictions for drunkenness followed thick and fast . . . . Joseph Thomas dismissed after nine months ; William Todd (ex 1st King's Dragoon Guards) after six months ; Thomas Birch (ex 4th Light Dragoons, a participant in the charge up Penlan Hill and in the rescue of Henry Westlake)[2] after a year ; and David Woolcock ("Reform" rioter and ex-gaolbird) after four years. Others resigned in anticipation . . . Robert Awberry (of the Talog expedition) after five years and Henry Thomas (ex Water Street gatekeeper) after only seven months.

And all this in a force of six constables !

One way or another James Hill George had to go if discipline was to be restored, but in a decision it was to regret, the Watch Committee merely demoted him to Inspector as a makeshift arrangement[3] and advertised in the *Times*, the *Bristol Mercury* and the Carmarthen and Swansea newspapers for a new Chief Constable at the considerably enhanced salary of £120 a year—half as much again as they were paying George. They were looking for a professional, someone who would put the seal of respectability on the little force, now comparing very unfavourably with its new, well-disciplined county neighbour under its martinet Chief Constable.

The Mayor and his Watch Committee were somewhat overwhelmed when the applications were placed before them :

> "There were no less than fifty-seven applications of every rank and grade, from the simple clerk (' of gentlemanly deportment, 6' 1½" in height', and who amongst other qualifications could ' ride a horse '), to a Baronet of High Degree, and an ample number of others of intermediate stations—a Colonel, Majors and Captains in the Army (including the Spanish Legion and the Irish Lancers), Lieutenants in the Army and the Navy, Commanders in the Navy and a host of ' Gentlemen '

of no present occupations, with a number of Superintendents and Sergeants of police, and others now in or formerly belonging to the police." (C.J.)

Their choice fell on Samuel Kentish, a native of Ferryside serving in the force at Defynnog, close to Sennybridge in Breconshire, and it proved to be a wise one, for Samuel Kentish was to serve the Borough for twenty-two years to his retirement in 1870. Although disciplinary problems were by no means swept away overnight and there would be no shortage of drunken policemen in Carmarthen for many years more, his appointment was a watershed in the history of the force, which from then on was firmly supervised and regulated. Carmarthen had seen its last ineffectual Chief Constable.

During the meeting which appointed him, Samuel Kentish heard something of the problem facing him, when—

> "A conversation took place on the disgraceful scenes enacted every Saturday night and Sunday morning, by the public houses being allowed to remain open, but it was agreed on all hands that until the new Chief Constable assumed his duties it was useless to say anything, as it was quite hopeless to expect any improvement under the present management." (C.J.)

Shortly afterwards he applied to the Watch Committee for an increase in the force from six to seven (which was granted), and he saw one of his men promoted Sergeant (at sixteen shillings (80 pence) a week) in place of John Hill George. Unlucky Frederick Rees missed this promotion by a hair's breadth, when it was given to an equally competent policeman, John Davies . . . *because he could read and write*, a decided advantage for a Sergeant !

During the deliberations on the proposed increase, Kentish remarked that his men worked from twelve to fifteen hours a day, *seven days a week*, and that he calculated the total distance walked by each man during a day's duty at about twenty miles. But it was "early days", and he had clearly not included in his calculations an allowance for time spent in pubs. He was soon to know better. For example, he soon had Nicholas Martin before the Watch Committee—

Carmarthen, 1884, with a ship under construction on the Pothouse Quay

"... for having been drunk at about half past twelve o'clock on the previous Wednesday morning, when he saw him sitting on the steps of a blacksmith's shop in a helpless state of inactivity.

Martin admitted the complaint and stated that, feeling rather unwell and fearing Cholera was coming on, he accepted the invitation of a French sea-captain to take a glass of something warm, but added he (in his Irish brogue), 'I confess my irrer, yer honours, and if ye'll forgive me this one time I promise yer honours I'll never do it again, faith that I won't.'" (C.J.)

They forgave him, with a caution that next time, if *all* the inhabitants of the town petitioned in his favour it would do him no good, as he would be dismissed.[4] This was in the same week of 1849 that the town magistrates renewed the licences of *one hundred and thirty* public houses.

Nicholas Martin's faith in the medicinal efficacy of "something warm" was his defence to many of his forty-four disciplinary charges, including one in November, 1852, when Mayor Morris and the Watch Committee met—

"... to investigate a charge of drunkenness preferred against P.C. Nicholas Martin. Mr. Superintendent Kentish stated that on the previous Sunday night at 11 o'clock Sergeant Davies, in going through Lammas Street, saw Martin lying down in the street in a helpless state of intoxication. He was then removed to his residence. He wore his uniform.

Martin did not appear before the Committee, but forwarded to it a letter and a medical practitioner's certificate of his inability to attend on account of illness. The letter was long and facetious, and was evidently the production of a 'Wag' at Martin's expense (Martin could neither read nor write). It alleged that the 'Unfortunate Officer' had been induced to take a little brandy medicinally 'For his stomach's sake' and that *he had been eight months a disciple of father Matthew.*"[5] (C.J.)

Once again, in view of Martin's seventeen years faithful service (something unique in a force which lost most of its men within weeks or months through drunkenness) the Committee was lenient "although greatly displeased with his conduct".

Constable Thomas Burnhill (son of the ex-Governor of the County Gaol) lasted only two years and received his marching orders after an escapade with Constable William Jones in Saint Peter's Street. Burnhill was charged before the Watch Committee with "having wantonly and maliciously removed the signboard of the ' Royal Exchange ' public house", at about five o'clock one morning, and Jones was charged with assisting him. Burnhill's novel defence was that—

> " . . . on the morning in question, in company with P.C. Jones he had been reporting himself to the Sergeant and, feeling very chilly, he thought to take a glass of warmed ale, and as he was passing by the ' Royal Exchange ', where he was as intimate as in his own house, he tapped the signboard three times with his walking stick for the purpose of arousing the inmates. The board being very loose fell down on his arm. Hearing some footsteps he and P.C. Jones ran away, but soon afterwards returned to inform the landlord of what had happened, but before they had come back some other person had been there and taken the board into the house." (C.J.)

Of course, it was possible that publicans waited up until five o'clock in the mornings, just in case a passing policeman might need a "glass of warmed ale", but the Watch Committee did not think so. They sacked him. As for P.C. Jones, he survived the hearing, to remain a solid, reliable (though frequently wayward) Bobby for another thirty years—*the first Carmarthen P.C. to serve long enough to draw a pension.*

At the soul-searching meetings of the Watch Committee during periods of instability and indiscipline in the force in the 1840s, Councillor Morse was a persistent critic of the police. He it was who wanted the appointment of the new Borough Chief Constable to be made by the District Military Commander Colonel Love, instead of by the Watch Committee ; he it was who challenged a new Chief Constable's salary of £80 a year

(£1.53 a week) as being too high, and he it was who had said publicly that Miles Davies (a Sergeant) was no more fit to be a policeman than he (Councillor Morse) was to be Prime Minister of England. He was a real thorn in the side of the town's policemen, and one can imagine their delight when this pillar of rectitude was hoisted on the Ceffyl Pren !

The *Carmarthen Journal*, for some reason mystified at the non-intervention of the police, reported that—

> "For the last few nights the streets of Carmarthen have been the scene of confusion with the assembly of a great number of people who appeared anxious to try their hands at getting up a procession, but their hero *being too modest* to suffer his real self to be chaired round the town, they were obliged to be contented with carrying his effigy.
>
> Last night the streets were again disturbed by the same proceedings and the effigy was finally burned at the upper end of Spilman Street.
>
> Mr. Morse addressed the mob and observed that if they had no consideration for his feelings, yet they might for the persons who were in the house ; that he had not run away with another man's wife, nor seduced anyone's daughter, and a good deal more to the same effect.
>
> It is to be hoped that the people have the good sense to let the matter drop. If they have not, *the authorities should interfere.*" (C.J.)

Such an affair as this could count on a huge following from among the town's drunkards, who also trooped through the courts with clockwork regularity, none more so than the people of the riverside—the fishermen, the coraclemen and the sailors. One altercation among them, near the Quay, provoked angry criticism from the Watch Committee when—

> "Mr. W. Morris called the attention of the Chief Constable to a circumstance that augured badly for the discipline in the force. On Sunday morning between one and two o'clock, some drunken sailors and fishermen were creating a disturbance in Quay Street. There was

a policeman with them pretending to take them into custody, *but he was so drunk that he could hardly stand* !" (C.J.)

In contrast, James Kenny, a sailor, found the police very obliging when he was drunk and disorderly in King Street on a Sunday afternoon :

> "About one o'clock, just as people were leaving Church, defendant was seen in a beastly state of intoxication, crying out most lustily ' Watchman ; Police !' The policeman very shortly answered to the call . . . and conveyed him to the station-house." (C.J.)

John Lewis, known as John Swllt (or shilling), one of the coraclemen, received equally good service from Constable John Davies, who—

> " . . . was on duty in King Street at about half past twelve on Sunday morning, when he heard the defendant shouting out and making a great noise. He followed him up as far as Saint Peter Street, where he got still more noisy and called out at the top of his voice ' Where are the police now they are wanted ?' His questions were for his sake rather too speedily answered as Davies came up and, concurring in opinion with him that the police *were* wanted, laid his hand on his shoulder and walked him off to the station-house, where he was left ' Alone in his glory ' to cogitate on the events of the night." (C.J.)

But Lewis showed a rather more violent side of himself in a monumental punch-up one Sunday evening when Davies, now a Sergeant, fell in with him again in Lammas Street, where Lewis was—

> " . . . very drunk, cursing and swearing and very disorderly. Having refused to go home, he was taken in charge and the policeman attempted to take him to the station-house. He, however, resisted greatly and violently assaulted him. He endeavoured to trip up the officer and failing this he kicked him about the legs

92

several times, so much so that he was black and blue and his legs were greatly lacerated. He then struck him several times, spat in his face and at length got the officer's hand in his mouth and bit it very severely, and no doubt would have bitten a piece out of it if it had not been for a woman who took hold of him by the hair of his head.

After this, he got his hand between the officer's stock (tunic collar) and throat and would have choked him but for the fact that the hooks of the coat gave way. He also tore the officer's coat and cape, but at length, with the assistance of P.C. Rees, he was taken to the station-house, where he again kicked the officer several times and tore his cape so much that it was now quite worthless. They were obliged to use their truncheons." (C.J.)

Lewis' mate, William Thomas, another coracleman, tried to help him, and was charged with resisting Constable Frederick Rees in the execution of his duty and threatening to take away his life. P. C. Rees told the court that Thomas " . . . came on in a fighting attitude and, holding up his fists, said ' Damn you ; if you strike the man again I'll knock your brains out.' "

Another battle, in Water Street, shows the breadth of the town's drinking habits, occurring as it did at *ten o'clock on a Sunday morning*[6] when Constable Frederick Rees—

" . . . saw David Morgan lying down on the pavement quite drunk and creating a disturbance. The officer spoke to him, when he got up and immediately caught hold of him by the throat and struck him in the eye and on his breast and still held him by the throat, almost choking him, which obliged the policeman to use his truncheon." (C.J.)

On the way to the station-house with their prisoner, Constables Rees and Nicholas Martin encountered William Jones who, near the Ceffyl Du (Black Horse) public house[7] in Water Street—

" . . . caught hold of the collar of Morgan's coat and endeavoured to take him out of the custody of the police. Jones collected a great crowd there, and Martin received several kicks on the legs." (C.J.)

The *Carmarthen Journal*, condemning such interventions by the mob said—

> "These attacks upon the police have been too frequent, and we invariably note that the ' mobocracy ' generally take part with the accused, however deserving he is of the lock-up." (C.J.)

But when drink was in, sense was out, and some hefty beatings were taken by the police . . . though the stabbing of Constable John Davies was very exceptional. On a Monday night in 1848 he arrested David Davies for being drunk and disorderly and fought hard with him every inch of the way from Goose Street to the station house. Battered and bruised, the officer went home and undressed—

> " ' . . . but on laying myself down in bed I felt a smarting pain in my left arm, and on examination I found that I had been cut in the left arm and in the left side of the breast, and there were also cuts in my coats and shirt corresponding with the same. I was not aware of having been wounded until I laid myself down to rest.' Witness then showed to the magistrates the wounds on his person as well as the corresponding holes in his clothes." (C.J.)

A knife found on the prisoner was produced in court, but though David Davies was fined for drunkenness, the magistrates for some reason found the case of stabbing "not made out".

Not long after this case, we find John Davies, now a sergeant, having to enlist the aid of *six men* to take David Jones (alias Dai Doleth) from the Cressely public house in King Street to the station house in Cambrian Place. Sergeant Davies received a goodly number of bruises in that particular encounter, something which was all in a day's work to the policemen of Carmarthen in the nineteenth century.

But even drunkenness and violence could have its humorous side, as can be seen from the report of a "Pensioner's antipathy" in December, 1845. The old soldier had fought with Wellington against Napoleon's Frenchmen, and he adopted a novel defence when he was before the magistrates for being "outrageously drunk" and "beating the police rather severely" :

> "In extenuation of his offence, the prisoner stated that he was wounded in action in several parts of the body and that a little liquor affected him. When drunk, his blood rose at the sight of a policeman, *whose uniform so much resembled that of a Frenchman that he could not resist the temptation of ' licking Frenchmen by proxy.'*[8]
> The magistrates were not quite satisfied with this excuse and fined him £5 or a month's imprisonment."
> (C.J.)

Another incident with a humorous (though to the character concerned a painful) twist, arose from the great success of two army recruiting parties in the town over a period of weeks. Now the clouds of inebriation were a more common cause than the thirst for military glory for their success, and many were those who in their "morning after" hangovers found themselves a shilling richer and bound unwillingly for a soldier's life, so one Carmarthen man hit on an idea :

> "A man better known by the cognomen of ' Benny Hat Wen ' has this week *chopped the top off one of his fingers*, for the purpose of disabling him from being enlisted, being fearful that when under the influence of John Barleycorn he may give way to the bland and winning smiles of the ' Dashing Recruiting Sergeant ' and accept the proferred shilling.
> A short time ago he enlisted and when brought up for attestation (before the magistrates) pleaded drunkenness. He has since found that cutting off the finger is a sure and efficacious obstacle to his entering H. M. Service."
> (C.J.)

Any public entertainment which attracted the "lower orders" when they had imbibed could be counted on to end up in chaos, as did a "Nigger Entertainment"[9] held in a rented hall in the town, where a "general melee took place, and whistling, shouting, jumping, fighting and a ' variety of other entertainments ' ensued." The affair terminated in "riot and noise, the picquet (an army patrol) was sent for, the police were called in, and, as an appropriate finale, the services of the police were called in to oblige the organiser to pay for the room, a proceeding which it appears he forgot to do."[10] And the town's fairs were noisy, rip-roaring occasions, which attracted rogues from far and wide. In June, 1844, Henry Westlake, the town's "officious" Chief Constable, rounded up a bunch of Swansea pickpockets whom he found "going among the country people whenever they saw a crowd collected" :

> "Several others of the same craft immediately left the town when they saw how they would be likely to be dealt with. Two of the prisoners were sent to the House of Correction for a fortnight, and the other three for three weeks each, *and they were all ordered to have their hair close cropped*, which seemed to annoy them very much.
> Several others were charged with drunkenness and disorderly conduct on the night of the fair." (C.J.)

The numerous contemporary reports of rascality at the fairs include one which describes how—

> " . . . during the last week the town was visited by a lot of rascals dressed as sailors with long curling hair, who pretend to be smugglers, selling what they call ' Foreign glass ' at 'reduced prices '."

Doubtless the forefathers of some of the "cheap-jacks" who make fleeting appearances in Carmarthen's market to-day, a hundred and forty years or so later !

It is hardly surprising, given such a prevalence of drunkenness in the town, that efforts should have been made to turn the people away from drink, and it is a matter of history that the non-conformist movements achieved a great deal in that respect as the century wore on. Perhaps *total abstinence* was a bit too much to go for all at once, though, as the results of some such efforts show. For example, the *Carmarthen Journal*

Carmarthen Market in the 1850s

The King Street Assembly Rooms, 1858: " . . . a home for the Carmarthen Literary and Scientific Institution and facilities for entertainments . . . "

viewed such an extreme approach with disfavour when it reported in 1844 that—

> " . . . that villifying humbug, Scott, of teetotal notoriety gave, as he called it, a ' Lecture ' on teetotalism under the (Market) Cross in this town.
>
> What became of (the procession) afterwards we know not, except that *one of them found his way to the station house drunk*, in the course of the evening." (C.J.)

At a meeting held in the Guildhall for "the suppression of intemperance" before the 1847 election, R. Walkden Esquire, Gellideg, addressed those present—

> " . . . enforcing the necessity of putting an end to those disgraceful scenes of drunkenness and debauchery generally attendant on an election, *but the meeting was rather thinly attended* !" (C.J.)

Another unsuccessful effort was made in October, 1847, at a—

> " . . . public meeting to advocate total abstinence from intoxicating liquors, held in the Lancastrian schoolroom. *The attendance was very small.* Perhaps the uninviting character of the place selected for the meeting contributed in no small degree to this, as it was essentially requisite that the olefactory nerves of those present should not be over-sensitive, *for they could not tolerate the noxious exhalations emitted from the slaughterhouse beneath.*
>
> How the master and scholars of the Lancastrian School are able to stand the dire effluvium we cannot account for, except by the same reason as that given by the fisherwomen when skinning the eels . . . that ' They are used to it.' " (C.J.)

Sometimes, though, even the *Carmarthen Journal* gave up, and simply skated over the drunkenness and its attendant violence with the terse comment that—

> "The cases before the Magistrates at the Town Hall were entirely destitute of interest, *being merely drunkenness and disorderliness, which do not call for a Report.*" (C.J.)

As a busy little port, Carmarthen attracted prostitutes from far and wide, and the appearances of these "Nymphs of the Pave" before the magistrates provided the newspapers with much material for humorous treatment. Anne Awberry was a star performer, so often did she appear—and the magistrates lost count of how often :

> "Town Hall, 25th January, 1847 : Anne Awberry was brought up charged with being drunk and disorderly ' *as usual* ' on Sunday night. P.C. Frederick Rees proved that about twelve o'clock he was on duty in Lammas Street when he heard the defendant making a disturbance and cursing and swearing very much. It appeared that she only came out of gaol late on Sunday evening.
>
> She entered into a long defence, denying the charge and giving as a reason that she had been in Church on Sunday evening, and very indignantly asked ' *Do you think I could be so wicked as to get drunk after being in Church* ?'
>
> Her defence was not considered a good one and she was committed to the House of Correction for a month." (C.J.)

And three months later, after two further appearances—

> "Anne Awberry who, it would appear by her presence before Their Worships, had been once more released from gaol, seems by her conduct determined to return to her old quarters, being charged with being drunk and disorderly." (C.J.)

Continuing to pile up a list of convictions without parallel in Carmarthen—

> "Anne Awberry, who had been only a few days released from her Old Quarters in the gaol, was brought up on a charge of drunkenness and disorderly conduct.
>
> The prisoner prayed very earnestly for the magistrates to give her another trial, and she would certainly reform and become a better woman in her old age. The Mayor

said that as it was her first offence this year (*it was only the* 10*th of January* !) the bench would discharge her." (C.J.)

And several appearances later—

"Anne Awberry again ! ! ! The incorrigible Anne Awberry was again brought up and despatched to her Old Quarters for two months. She begged hard to be left off this time as she had only been at liberty since the previous Wednesday and she would be a good girl henceforth, but Their Worships were inexorable.

The Mayor said this was the fourteenth time of Anne's committal, and Mr. Morris said that it was nearly the hundred and fourteenth time ! *Anne went sprightly off in company with the Policeman to take her sojourn in the Stronghold.*" (C.J.)

One Nymph of the Pave really put the cat among the pigeons :

"Maria Thomas, a prostitute, was brought up upon the complaint of P.C. William Todd with having at a late hour on the previous night annoyed the inhabitants and made an uproar in the public streets.

In her defence she denied the statement of the policeman *and stated that he had made improper overtures to her*, which she having rejected, he took her to the station house.

She was removed to the gaol, where a little corrective discipline might have a good effect." (C.J.)

When Maria—"determined that at least once a week she must figure in the police court"—was, shortly afterwards, committed for another three months for being drunk and disorderly, the *Carmarthen Journal* commented wryly that—

" . . . for some time she will cease from troubling the authorities."

She could attract the crowds, too :

"P.C. Nicholas Martin deposed that on the previous day he saw defendant in Lammas Street. She was very drunk and surrounded by about a hundred people. She was cursing and swearing dreadfully. Martin endeavoured to take her to the station house, but she threw herself on her back on the ground and after some difficulty *she was taken to the station house on a truck*." (C.J.)

From as far away as Ireland they came, and there was a touch of poetic justice when Anne Wilkinson was arrested by fellow-countryman, Constable Nicholas Martin, who told Their Worships that—

> "She was in truth the worst character he had ever come across. To sum up, the officer, himself a native of ' Ould Eirrean', said ' Sure enough, your Honour, she is a disgrace to the Emerald Isle.'
>
> The defendant denied that she was drunk, and with a strong touch of the brogue added ' *Mr. Martin was a fitter candidate for the station house last night than I was.*' " (C.J.)

When dealing with women like these, Their Worships frequently pointed the moral finger at them as, for example, when—

> "A ' Nymph of the Pave', Mary Anne Thomas, one of the Frail Sisterhood, young in years though old in iniquity, was charged with being drunk and disorderly. The Mayor seriously admonished the prisoner on the disreputable life she was leading, and in discharging her *bade her ' Go and sin no more*'—an injunction which, we are afraid, will be disregarded." (C.J.)

A fairly close (at times *too* close) relationship between the town prostitutes and their tormentors, the police, is suggested by the experience of a commercial traveller who arrived by coach from Gloucester and—

> " . . . then went to a number of public houses and late at night ' Fell in with some girls of the town ' and about three o'clock in the morning he was staggering about the streets very drunk, and meeting with a policeman in Lammas Street he enquired for lodgings ' . . . where he could meet with some women of loose character', *and was shown to a brothel in Lammas Street* kept by

one Mary Howells, where he remained for the remaining part of the night in company with the prisoner (a prostitute charged with stealing gold sovereigns from his trousers, which he had hung over a chair !)" (C.J.)

The relationship between the "Nymphs" and the arm of the law reached its highest point in 1851 when the town became alive with rumour that one of the policemen, Thomas Phillips, had actually married one, and—scandal upon scandal—*she was said to have a husband already* ! And then . . . consternation :

"On Saturday morning last (the 1st of March, 1851) the greatest excitement prevailed among the populace, who had assembled in considerable crowds in the immediate neighbourhood of the Town Hall, in consequence of it becoming known that a female who had recently married one of the Borough Police of the name of Phillips, *had been taken into custody* by Mr. Kentish, the Chief Constable, under a warrant from the Mayor, charged with bigamy, and that she was to be brought up that morning.

All sorts of absurd rumours were exceedingly rife, and it was highly ludicrous and not a little amusing to witness the deep anxiety of the ' Ladies ' to catch a glimpse of one of their own sex who, it was affirmed, had succeeded in obtaining ' No less than four husbands ' while many of the ' Fair spectators ' were not sufficiently captivating to obtain even a single chance, and numerous were the railings at the fickle Godess in distributing her favours with such an unequal hand.

Great crowds assembled around the Town Hall to obtain a sight of the prisoner, and for some time Guildhall Square was almost impassable and a large concourse of people followed the prisoner to the Gaol." (C.J.)

In the same week, P.C. Phillips was called before the Watch Committee who heard how the Chief Constable had warned him to consider very carefully before marrying the girl, "of whom he had heard lurid stories from the Swansea police", but—

"The Mayor remarked that he imagined that Phillips' love was both ' Blind and Hot ' and the Watch Committee then resolved that he be allowed to resign his situation to save him the disgrace of being turned out of the force." (C.J.)

At the same hearing, Constable Williams Jones, *who kept a common lodging house*, was dealt with on a disciplinary charge of *harbouring females of bad character*, including Phillips' "Wife". There could hardly be a more explicit description of a brothel, but in those days it took more than brothel-keeping to lose one's job as a policeman !

Jones was allowed one month to get rid of his lodgers.

Mary Callis, Phillips' "Wife", was committed for trial, at which—

" . . . she amused herself by laughing at her husband, Richard Callis, and occasionally held up her hand towards him in a threatening attitude.

A very great crowd followed her to the County Gaol, on the steps of which the prisoner coolly turned around to the spectators, *thanked them for their attendance, and bounded into prison with all the agility of a young lady going down a country dance with an amiable partner.*" (C.J.)

At the next Assizes she received six months for her "great outrage on public morals".

Moral Outrage

Many of the cases coming before the magistrates throw an interesting light on some of the attitudes and punishments of the mid-nineteenth century. "Profaning the Sabbath", for example, would always arouse the wrath of the worthies on the bench, as it did in March, 1844, when three coraclemen, Thomas Williams, Thomas Joseph and John Lewis were sentenced to be "Exhibited in the public stocks for three hours" for profaning the Sabbath by "Assembling together and pursuing unlawful games on a Sunday, by playing what is called ' Pitch and Toss '."

Landlords of the town's one hundred and thirty public houses were frequently fined for "selling ale before the termination of Divine Service on a Sunday morning", and when some boys were brought up for *"playing marbles on the Quay on a Sunday"*—

> "The Mayor severely but justly commented upon and expressed his deep regret at the immorality of the youths of the Town, and he was of opinion that some measure ought to be adopted to put a stop to so fearful an evil."
> (C. J.)

Suicide was a crime and was regarded as the height of profanity. A report of September, 1848, shows how the rougher element of the town took full advantage of the Church's revenge on the suicide, and how—

> " . . . one of the most disgusting scenes witnessed in this Town for a long time took place. We allude to the burial without Funeral Rites of the body of a respectable old man named Jones who committed suicide.
>
> It having become known that the body was to be interred, a vast concourse of people amounting to some hundreds assembled to witness the sad sight, and when the coffin was brought out about nine o'clock, borne on the shoulders of four men, who galloped away with it almost at the top of their speed, the scene was truly disgraceful to a civilised and Christian nation, as the conduct of the populace, who occupied the time in coarse and indecent jesting, laughing and jeering and other more depraved acts, far more befitted a heathen than a civilised nation.
>
> The body having been brought into the Church yard, it was almost literally thrown into the grave and covered over with the greatest rapidity.
>
> If such scenes as these must be enacted, we think they may very easily be conducted in a more orderly manner and at a time when they are not likely to be attended by such truly demoralising accompaniments as characterised that on Thursday night." (C. J.)

A commentary on the state of the poor at that time is found

in an Editorial in the *Carmarthen Journal* which also carried a suggestion for a sort of "do-it-yourself" justice that might provide food for thought in our more "liberal" times :

> "As the inhabitants of this town already know, there are lots of idle vagabonds who, sooner than work to obtain an honest livelihood, commit petty offences *for the purpose of getting into gaol*, where the fare generally is much superior to what they ordinarily obtain. Now it is evident that committing these fellows to the House of Correction is worse than useless, it being attended by a heavy expense to the ratepayers.
>
> The advice therefore which we tender to the inhabitants is that offered by Mr. E. H. Stacey at the Magistrates' meeting, which is that whenever they catch one of these fellows ' up to his tricks ' as they call it, or breaking windows, *to lay hold of him and administer a sound, hearty, thrashing*, which will, we doubt not, have the desired effect." (C.J.)

Carmarthen's magistrates' court in the mid-1850s must have been an entertainment in itself. On one occasion in 1851, Captain John George Philipps, R.N. (the "Blue" candidate in the "Reform" elections of 1831), now getting on a bit, found himself sitting through a boring and pedantically defended case of "Gambling and Card-playing" against Jonah Harries, landlord of the Golden Keys public house. Sergeant Miles Davies was being cross-examined at interminable length and great play was being made by Mr. Parry, the defending solicitor, on the word "knowingly" as a necessary ingredient of the offence.

It went on, and on, and on, until suddenly the old sea dog lost his temper and roared "Oh, this is all nonsense. We shall be here a month if we listen to Mr. Parry's law. What are you going to do, Mr. Mayor ?" The Mayor said "Let us act calmly and dispassionately in an endeavour to do justice," to which the gallant Captain retorted ("angrily"), "Oh nonsense. Here is card-playing going on and the defendant is accountable for what takes place." From Mr. Parry : "Do you know what takes place in your kitchen?" From Captain Philipps ("passionately") : "Yes I do (a pause), at least I ought to do !"

"The whole court was convulsed with laughter. ' Silence ' roared out Sergeant Davies in a voice of thunder and a face as red as an angry turkey-cock. Captain Philipps (evidently out of temper) cried ' Turn those fellows out ; turn them out directly.' After some further conversation between the Mayor and Captain Philipps, the latter rose from his seat and in an excited manner said ' I'm not going to sit here a month.' The Honourable magistrate then hastily left the court." (C.J.)

The Mayor, now alone, dismissed the case.

Transportation still appeared regularly in the sentences handed down at the Assizes in the Guildhall. In July, 1848, for instance, Thomas Corcey Adams, a London con-man, was convicted of obtaining £164 from the Carmarthen bankers, Wilkins and Company, on a forged bill of exchange. The judge sentenced him to *transportation for fourteen years*, after which he reminded Adams that only a few years previously he would have "*forfeited his life*" for such an offence.

No doubt there were many in those days, too, who complained that the law was becoming soft on the criminal !

In another "Transportation" case in October, 1844, a familiar figure reappeared in Carmarthen, when Evan Lewis, a mason of the town, known as "Evan Clary", was convicted of stealing *two blankets* from the Carmarthen Union Workhouse, and sentenced *to be transported to Australia for seven years*. Before passing sentence the judge heard evidence of a previous conviction and sentence, given by none other than *Mr. John Lazenby*, now the Governor of Brecon County Gaol, last heard of eight years before when the new "Blue" Town Council had turned him out of office as Chief Constable of Carmarthen. And prosecuting counsel was *George Thomas*, junior, son of Lazenby's old adversary of the "Reform" election of thirteen years before !

It is truly a small world, but the prisoner, understandably, found little comfort in that, for though he—

" . . . received the sentence very coolly, he observed that he would return to his Native Town at the expiration of his sentence *and would have the pleasure of dancing over George Thomas's and Jack Lazenby's graves* !" (C.J.)

NOTES

1So described by Alcwyn Evans (Nat. Lib. of Wales Ms. 12368E).

2Over the years a number of soldiers stationed in the town stayed to join the force when their time expired. Since the army rank and file—largely recruited from the dregs of society—were notoriously drunken, it is not surprising that there was so much of it in the force.

3In that rank he was disciplined for drunkenness and survived for only one month. Even afterwards he was before the magistrates for drunkenness and assault.

4Martin had already been reinstated on the petition of a number of the townspeople after being dismissed for drunkenness.

5Father Matthew was the famous architect of a teetotal movement in Ireland which was reputed to have cut whisky consumption there from $12\frac{1}{4}$ million gallons to $5\frac{1}{4}$ gallons in four years. A report of 1853 however, connected his absence in America with the increase of whisky consumption to $8\frac{1}{2}$ million gallons, or 10 pints per person (including the large child population) per year !

6The police regularly kept observations on public houses as early as seven o'clock on Sunday mornings !

7Still open for business in 1980.

8The British had last fought the French thirty years ago—at Waterloo.

9A "Nigger Minstrels" show, extremely popular in the U.S.A. and Britain at that time (1848) in which the performers blacked their faces. The television version of that style of entertainment was the BBC's show "The Black and White Minstrels."

10*Carmarthen Journal.*

CHAPTER SEVEN

TURNING POINTS

THE half-way point of the century saw the coming together of a number of influences which had fundamental significance for Carmarthen. The cholera epidemic of 1849, which carried off a hundred and two people out of three hundred and fifty-four known cases in Carmarthen, marked a turning point (albeit a long-drawn-out one) in attitudes to public hygiene;[1] the emergence from economic depression marked the real beginning of the long climb of the labouring classes out of the pit of poverty and ignorance; and the disappearance of the worst of the political violence from Carmarthen's streets after the purging of Rebecca's grievances brought a more civilised air to the town, as violence became the almost exclusive preserve of the fishermen, sailors and labouring classes—well within the capacity of the town's police.

But another development was of even greater significance to the town, to its prosperity, to the mobility of its people and—in the longer term—to its very character. The railway arrived in 1852, the first, ceremonial, train being greeted with great popular acclaim and every ounce of Carmarthen's special brand of exuberance. And, although it was not immediately apparent to the townspeople, Carmarthen's days as a port were numbered. The long decline towards the departure of the last little coastal steamer from the River Towy began on the day the last spike was driven into the last railway sleeper, within sight and sound of the ship-lined quay.

But the arrival of the railway was not without trauma. Any major construction project—even to-day—brings problems to the area which receives its labouring work-force, but the problems were vastly greater in the railway age, particularly during the early boom, when millions of tons of earth and rock had to be removed from deep cuttings and laid again as causeways across wide valleys and around steep sea walls by no other means than the shovels of the "Navigators", or "Navvies" as they became known. Huge crowds of English, Welsh and (mostly) Irish-emigrant labourers worked like ants on the track and the advanced earthworks, while horses and carts in their hundreds moved the debris to the embankments and spoil heaps.

As the railhead moved, so did the tents and shanties which formed the rowdy, often riotous railhead townships, where drink in abundance provided an escape from the hardships and privations of a "navvy's" life . . . and brought out the worst in the illiterate, hard-fighting drunkards among them. There had been skirmishes in and around Carmarthen since 1848, but in December, 1851, the railhead at Ferryside exploded in its full fury :

> "*Riot at the Ferryside—fight between English[2] and Irish navvies—nine men stabbed* : On Saturday night (the 6th of December) about midnight, a most disgraceful riot was created at the Ferryside by navvies employed on the railway line in that neighbourhood. Several persons unhesitatingly attribute the whole riot to a pot-house squabble.
>
> Great animosity and jealousy have long existed between the Irish and the English (sic) navvies, and an opportunity was only wanted to develop these bad feelings in their worst forms. Pokers, large pieces of timber, handles of brushes, knives and weapons of every description were used with determination to do the greatest possible injury, in a pitched battle between at least *a hundred and fifty* English and Irish navvies. Nine persons were stabbed and we are left to imagine how many were otherwise injured.
>
> On Monday, the English, about two hundred in number, drove away from the village every Irishman except two. A large number of them have since been lounging about the streets of this town in a state of great destitution as they have no work to do." (C.J.)

There followed, in subsequent reports, a long catalogue of arson, stabbings and beatings, as the Irish were burned out of their lodgings and pursued from the railhead, in scenes reminiscent of the wild townships of the Gold Rush, then in full swing in California. The disturbances continued on and off through the following two weeks, and they were finally quelled only by the swearing in of fifty special constables, including a number of men from Carmarthen town, though the navvies would remain troublesome in their progress across West Wales for a few more years yet.

History was made at about half past one in the afternoon of Monday the 6th of September, 1852, when a vast crowd witnessed the arrival in Carmarthen of the very first engine to traverse the single track fom Swansea :

> "It approached the station at the rate of *fifteen miles an hour*,[3] drawing after it several trucks containing materials for the building of the station, and four or five gentlemen. After unloading the trucks, the train returned to the Ferryside—a distance of six miles and a half in nine minutes (an average speed of *more than forty-three miles an hour* !)" (C.J.)

There followed in quick succession the beginning of the first regular train service to Swansea and the east, and the extension of the line westward to Haverfordwest, each of these events being accompanied by great public celebration. It was the end of Carmarthen's comparative isolation, and the town would never be the same again.

As a force for the emancipation of the town or village-tied common man, the impact of the railway was immense, and within a year or two a look back at pre-railway times was a look back into a remote age . . . to the time of burly stage-coachmen and gaily attired guards, whose "shrill horns waked the echoes of many silent spots and the slumbers of many a somnolent gatekeeper, when the maximum speed in travelling was obtainable only in one of those conveyances ' licensed to carry four inside and eight out.' The ' Good old Coaching Days ' as they are wont to be designated are well-nigh reckoned as things of the past."[4]

This was truly a turning point. "A Great and Important Event."[5]

On the morning of Friday the 21st of July, 1854—in the year of the outbreak of the Crimean War—gentleman's groom David Williams travelled by train from his native Narberth to Carmarthen, and walked across the river bridge and up Bridge Street to the town centre. He had an appointment at the Guildhall.

Twenty-five years old, five feet nine inches and a strong-framed, fresh-faced, blue-eyed country lad, his ambition was to don the tailcoat and top hat of a policeman. In the entrance hall he met Richard Lewis, already a policeman, who had applied to transfer to the eight-man Carmarthen Borough Police Force. Both were accepted and within a couple of days they were patrolling the streets of the town, to earn sixteen shillings (80p) for a fifteen-hour day and seven-day week. Their fellow constables were another recent recruit, John Davies of Llanboidy, two-year man Henry James, station-house keeper William Woozley (five years service) and the redoubtable Nicholas Martin, the only remaining founder-member of the force of 1836. Thomas Buckley was their Sergeant.

David Williams came to Carmarthen at a time of unprecedented prosperity and development in the town, which had made a quite remarkable break with the violence of its recent past. True there was still a great deal of drunkenness and fighting among the "lower orders", particularly along the riverside among the fishermen and the Irish immigrants,[6] but the "Carmarthen Mob"—the genuine article, *à la* 1831 and 1843 —had evaporated in the sunshine of political and social reform and the new prosperity.

While the poor were still poor, the gulf was narrowing, though relief funds and soup kitchen handouts were still regular features of the winter months, as they would be right through to the twentieth century.

A far greater proportion of the townspeople than ever before found nourishment within their reach, even though most of them had to work exceedingly long hours to earn the money for it.

The Sunday Schools flourished and the various religious de-nominations of the town contributed to the charities which ran schools like the "Lancastrian" in Pentrepoeth,[7] where two hundred and seven boys and a hundred and fifty-three girls learned their "Three Rs" and a respect for their elders under a strict but benevolent discipline.

Social occasions were no longer the exclusive preserve of the "gentry" ; the season of 1856/57 saw three "Tradesmen's Balls" held at the Boar's Head, the first of their kind. The thirst for knowledge and culture among the "Mechanics", tradesmen and the middle-class was catered for by such institutions as Mr. Shackells's "Library and Reading Room" in Lammas Street, the setting for lectures on the widest range of subjects by eminent visitors, and the King Street Assembly Rooms, which provided a home for the "Carmarthen Literary and Scientific Institution" and facilities for entertainments ranging from the Carmarthen Hunt Ball to performances by travelling opera and theatrical companies, to choral society concerts, to lectures. The King Street theatre was redecorated "in an elegant and comfortable style" and the proceedings there were conducted with a decorum unknown in the recent past.

Elections still aroused feverish excitment and rivalry in the town, as indeed they still do, but gone were the violent scenes and army bayonets which had characterised the contests of past years.

But Christmas Eve could still be counted on to be the wildest night of the year, perpetuating at least one facet of the town's "Wild Western" character. Blazing tar barrels, torch proces-sions, street explosions and pistol-firing horsemen marked the arrival in Carmarthen of the "Festive Season" in the tradition of "Torch Night", a tradition which only finally burned itself out in 1870, when the Mayor forbade it.

Yes, Carmarthen still had its wild moments, and there were still battles to be fought in its streets. David Williams and his fellow recruit were briefed by their battle-hardened colleagues as they were shown through the confusing network of narrow streets, steps and passages in their initiation into the town : "Patrol in pairs through Chequers Alley, along the Quay and through Dan y Banc and Kidwelly Fach beyond the bridge ; when tackling the Lewises, keep one eye over your shoulder for the Thomases, the Evanses and the Eliases ;[8] tread carefully when you're called to a coracle family fight. They have a nasty way of joining forces against outsiders who interfere in family business !"

David Williams' duty diary—a rare survivor from those days[9]—gives us a glimpse of his life on the beat, and a lively entry for Christmas Day shows only too clearly that "Torch Night" was by no means simply a wild prelude to a quiet and peaceful religious festival :

> "Saturday, Christmas Day, 1858. Attended at the Guildhall at 10.30 a.m. and accompanied the whole of the Force into Saint Peter's Church in procession before the Mayor, W. H. Norton, Esquire. Returned at 1.15 p.m. Resumed duty at 9 p.m. at the station house.
>
> At 11 p.m. assisted in locking up John Curtis, rag dealer, Kidwelly Fach, charged with dangerously wounding Bridgett Driscoll of near the Parade. At 2.20 a.m. P.C. Edwards and myself locked up John Williams, 17, son of ' Dickie ' and John Davies, 17, son of ' Bogus', charged with being drunk and disorderly in Nott Square and Bank Lane. Also Sergeant Beynon, P.C.s. Woozley and James locked up Evan Jones, Paper Mills, and William Evans, Cambrian Place, both charged with being drunk and fighting in Lammas Street. Also there had been fighting on Picton Terrace at 1.30 a.m., and the wife of John Rees, mariner, Quay, had been assaulted by some person at 12.15 a.m. when near the ' Angel ' public house in Lammas Street. Remained on duty till 6 a.m."

In that year Christmas Day fell on a Saturday, a day which throughout the year was the high point of the Carmarthen drinking week. On another Saturday night, David Williams—

> " . . . commenced duty at 9 p.m. to the station-house. Cleared out a *Cwrw bach*[10] in Dame Street at 1 a.m. Also at 1.10 a.m. turned out some parties from the house of Mary Anne Thomas, Chequers Alley. About 1.20 a.m.

St. Peter's Church in 1858

The Fusilier Monument, unveiled on 20th September, 1858. The 23rd Regiment
chose Carmarthen for this unique memorial because the first soldier killed at the
battle of the Alma was a Carmarthen man—from Friar's Park

Carmarthen Bridge in the 1850s

I was standing in company with P.Sgt. Beynon and P.C. Evans when we heard a noise from Chequers Alley. We went there and found by the door of Mary Anne Thomas, Thomas Dolan, navvy, Thomas Thomas, miner of Pen y Danan, Glamorganshire, Lemuel Thomas, weaver of Tanerdy, all of them engaged in fighting and making a row. We took them all into custody.

I then returned to the Square. John Rees, blacksmith, desired me between 2 and 3 a.m. to come to his house as George Lewis, shoemaker, would not leave. I seen all quiet within and then came outside and ordered the crowd to disperse who was at the door. They were all in the act of moving off except John Griffiths, weaver, Blue Street, who was drunk. He moved on for a few yards but then said that ' By damned, he would not go any further for the damned bugger.' I then caught hold of him to move him off. He then struck me several times in my face until it was covered with blood. He also kicked me and P.C. Evans. I used my staff in self-defence. He was very violent on the way to the Station-house."

And on another Saturday :

"I went on duty this day at 10 a.m. to the Priory Street beat until 12.30 p.m. I then relieved to dinner P.C. Woozley on the King Street beat until 1.40 p.m.

I resumed duty at 9 p.m. to the King Street beat at 9.45 p.m. I had to turn out Thomas Jones, alias ' Sir Hugh ' from the house of Mr. Collard (the Markets Superintendent). About 12.45 a.m. after P.C. Woozley had returned from Priory Street, we were together at the corner of Queen Street when we heard much screaming towards Castle Green. We immediately went there and found James Davies, miner of Shaws Lane, Thomas Jones, sawyer of Dan y Banc, John Jones, cabinet maker of Castle Green, David Thomas, labourer of Castle Green, Thomas Davies, nailer of Dan y Banc, and John Thomas, shoemaker of Castle Green—all of them fighting.

Finding that we could not take all at once into custody, we separated them from each other to get the place clear. While endeavouring to take James Davies to his house, he went to strike me but was prevented by his wife and a young lad and his sister. He then became more violent and P. C. Woozley went to persuade him to go home with his wife. He then caught hold of Thomas Davies and struck P.C. Woozley in the face. We then caught hold of him and was obliged to restrain him as he resisted all that was in his power. We dragged him some few yards and I took out my truncheon, as there were several persons there who I thought would try to rescue him from our custody. We then had the assistance of Sgt. Lewis and P.C. Beynon and we carried him up Bridge Street and took him to the Station-house.

I patrolled the beat to and fro during the remainder of the night till 6 a.m. Found all correct—fine Weather."

David Williams had done twelve hours and forty minutes duty, spread over twenty hours, and he would be back on duty within four hours. At an hourly rate of 1p! Even when special duties intervened, they were not allowed to affect the hours of duty demanded. For example—

"I commenced duty this day at 9 a.m. to the Lammas Street beat till 10 a.m., about which time I had orders to proceed to the Workhouse to take and convey Bridgett Connolly and her two children to Waterford in Ireland. I left the Carmarthen Station at 12.30 p.m., arriving at Neyland about 3 p.m. then left Neyland in the 'Mallakoff' steamship, arriving at Waterford at 8 p.m. Thursday the 25th.

Next day proceeded about 4 p.m. in the 'Mallakoff', arriving at Neyland about 12.30 a.m. Proceeded at 5 a.m. from Neyland by train, arriving at Carmarthen at 6.45 a.m. Reported myself to P.C. Davies at 7 a.m. in Lammas Street. Also reported myself to my Superintendent (Chief Constable) about 9.30 a.m.

I then went on duty at 12.30 p.m. to the Lammas Street beat until 2 p.m., resuming duty at 3.30 p.m.

to the same beat until 5 p.m. Then to tea until 5.30 p.m., then to the same beat until 9 p.m. Found all correct."

Sixty hours out of eighty-four !

The rank of Sergeant brought no relief in the long hours required of a policeman ; nor did family tragedy, as Sergeant Williams found in July, 1859, when he was allowed one hour and twenty minutes off "in consequence of my little child being very ill". Next day he was allowed four and a half hours off "in consequence of my child died this morning at 3.30 a.m". and, two days later—three hours "*to bury my child*".

But David Williams' devotion to his duty never flagged over the whole of his thirty-four years service, though even he had the Carmarthen policeman's traditional partiality to the jug . . . with twenty-five disciplinary appearances to prove it ! But he was the first Sergeant to serve long enough to draw a pension, and in so doing he set a new standard of loyalty and dedication, which was followed by almost all of his successors in the rank. The service of his predecessors had ranged from one year to four, and most had been dismissed for disciplinary offences or resigned when they saw the writing on the wall.

As a Sergeant (after four years service) he supervised his men assiduously, his duty record sparing none of their derelictions, and yet always showing an understanding of their weaknesses:

> "When I first saw P.C. Arthur at 12.30 a.m. he appeared to be under the influence of liquor. I went to Pendre to meet him a little after 1 a.m. He was gossipping with two men. He was much under the influence of liquor at that time, but during the night he came better and remained on duty till 6 a.m."

*   *   *

> "At 11.45 p.m. I went to visit P.C. Griffiths on the Lammas Street beat. Not finding him there I listened at the door of the 'Coopers Arms'.[11] I then went inside and told him to come out, for shame. He then pretended to unbuckle his belt and pretended that he had only been

in there doing his business *at the privy.* I told him that
would never do."

*   *   *

"I then noticed P.C. Evans under the influence of
liquor and told him that he ought to be ashamed of
himself, as it is not only a few days ago since Thomas
No. 8 was dismissed. He said nothing more then and I
told him for to be sure to mind not to sit down and fall
asleep.

At about 1.40 a.m. I went to the house of P.C. Jones,
and lying down in the passage I found P.C. Evans
quite fast asleep. I aroused him so well as ever I could
and I took him down to his beat and cautioned him
again to take care of himself and mind to go his rounds
regular."

*   *   *

There were times, of course, when things went too far :
"At 12 midnight I found P.C. D. Thomas coming
from the ' Coopers Arms '. He was then under the
influence of liquor. I sent him round his beat at 12.40
a.m. Not finding him, I went in search for him with
P.C. Griffiths at 1 a.m. and we found him lying down
near the house of Anne Davies, alias ' Nancy Cap Du'[12] a
Brothel in Pendre. We got him up and tried to get him
to walk, but he was so drunk that he could scarcely
stand up on his feet. We then took him home and undressed him, after which he became so very violent that
he struck at me. P.C. Griffiths then caught hold of him
and we then left him and went to the Superintendent
and reported the whole of it."

*   *   *

"P.Cs. James and Arthur reported to me that P.C.
John Thomas was very drunk this night and that he
assaulted P.C. James whilst preventing him from assaulting his wife."

*   *   *

116

Race Week was a particularly trying period of temptation for the constables ; since drunkenness was the order of the day on the course and in the town, it would have taken better men than them to say "No !". For instance :

> "At 12 noon proceeded with the P.Cs. to the Race-course[13] remaining there till 5.45 p.m., then returned and met the Superintendent at the corner of Water Street. P.C. Griffiths did not return to town with us. He appeared under the influence of liquor.
>
> I then resumed duty at 10 p.m. in best uniform to the Assembly Rooms, there being a Ball to-night, which passed off quiet and terminated at 4 a.m."

*   *   *

> "Attended at the Station-house this day at 11.45 a.m. then to the racecourse, returning about 7 p.m. P.C. James was very drunk on the way home. The Superintendent was present at the time and sent him off down to Johnstown.
>
> I then went on duty to the Assembly Rooms as there was a Ball there which terminated at 5.20 a.m. P.Cs Powell and Thomas returned from Johnstown at 1.45 a.m. Thomas was then very drunk. He became better by the time I discharged the P.Cs."

And Then There Were Twelve

David Williams was still a constable in 1857 when the Borough Force at last reached a strength of twelve—and became the legendary "Carmarthen Shilling". There would be twelve "Coppers" in Carmarthen for the next eighty years.

Through the 1850s and 1860s—and indeed into the twentieth century—the "Carmarthen Shilling" dealt manfully with its task of clearing the rowdy streets, and David Williams' diary echoes the sound of the fray :

> "There was a *bidding*[14] at the 'Angel' Inn, Lammas Street, this day. I was called there several times during

the afternoon to stop rows there between some of the Cornish miners and others.

I was standing at the corner of Water Street near the new Monument[15] in company with P.C. Evans No. 6, when we was called to the 'Angel' Inn, Lammas Street, to turn out some Irish who were making a row and breaking all that came near them. We went in there and in a passage found Michael Donaghue, Daniel Cooney, James Driscoll in a scuffle with the landlord and his father-in-law. We went in and took them out to the street and requested them to go off. They refused and became more violent and cursing and swearing very bad. I then took Michael Donaghue into custody and James Driscoll and Dan Cooney then attempted to rescue him from custody."

And it was not always the "lower orders" whose drunken behaviour demanded the attention of the police. All classes of the townspeople had their moments :

"At 2 a.m. I locked up George Tomlinson, *gentleman*, Spilman Street, charged with being drunk and disorderly in Guildhall Square. He was very insolent and wanted to fight and he had his two coats off."

*   *   *

"At 12.35 a.m. I assisted Mr. James Evans ' Who was very tipsy by the Assembly Rooms ', home, accompanied by Mr. Alcwyn Evans."[16]

*   *   *

"About 12.45 a.m. P.C. Jones No. 7 and I heard loud talking in the 'Vine' public house, and Captain Brown-Edwardes[17] came out from there and Mr. Protheroe of the National Bank. We went into the house and there saw Mr. W. J. Morgan, ' Welshman ' (newspaper) Office, Edgar Evans, David Lewis, Jnr., and W. Morgan Solicitor, E. H. Davies and Mr. Tamplin, the landlord.

All was under the influence of liquor and we left them there."[18]

There were many other duties to attend to besides tackling the town drunks and settling family quarrels. There were the very few cases of crime and criminals to be handled, the incredible traffic jams to be cleared and the "furious riders" chased and prosecuted, the quay to be kept clear of landed cargo, and (somewhat at odds with the general air of "drink and be merry") the publicans to be harried late at night and on Sundays, then, as now, "Dry" days. "Dry" the day might be, but "Dry" the pubs were not, because David Williams' diary and such police occurrence books as survive are liberally sprinkled with lists of public houses and the names of people—high as well as low—found in them on Sundays by the police !

And, of course, there were their duties for the Courts. Twice a year the pomp and circumstance of the Assize Judge's arrival had to be observed and this always provided a job for the police and a scene of pageantry and colour for the responsive townspeople, the Judge's carriage being met well outside town by the High Sheriff of the County, the Town Mayor and the Corporation, all in their colourful regalia. Huge crowds followed the procession, which was preceded by a half dozen or so men shouldering javelins, followed by numerous horsemen, banners and bands of music. The whole town would be *en fete* as the Judge, his court officials, the Mayor, the Corporation and the County "Gentry" proceeded to Saint Peter's Church for Divine Service, the preliminary to several days of pageantry surrounding the dispensation of the Queen's Justice by Her Judge of Assize.

The awe and respect accorded to this august personage by even the most lowly of the inhabitants of the town is one of the more marked contrasts with attitudes of the twentieth century. And one which speaks its own message.

It was in the magistrates' courts that most of Carmarthen's offenders were dealt with, including the few arrested for petty thefts, which no longer carried the savage sentences of yester-year. But "Savagery" is, of course, relative, and the experience of one young boy in 1856 illustrates, for example, the still wide gulf between the penal system of those days and modern attitudes towards juvenile offenders :

"John Llewellyn, a dirty looking lad *aged eight years*, was charged under the Juvenile Offenders Act with stealing money and several articles from the shop of Mrs. Llewellyn, Confectioner, King Street.

The boy's mother was in court and the magistrates censured her severely for not taking more care of her son. *He was committed to the house of correction for three calendar months, and to be once privately whipped.*" (C.J.)

As for the adults, a typical list of cases before the Mayor and his fellow magistrates in 1863 read thus : "P.C. John Beynon charged Jane Jones with drunkenness ; P.C. Morgan James charged David Jones, alias Dai Doleth, with drunkenness and assault; David Thomas charged Ebenezer Williams with assaulting him ; P. C. Thomas Evans charged Thomas Davies with drunkenness and assaulting the police ; Police Sergeant David James charged George Isaac with being drunk and riotous in the streets, and Henry Spressman with a like offence ; Mary Jones charged William Daniel with assaulting her, and—last but far from least—a name that first entered this story many years ago . . . Anne Awberry, the doyen of the town's drunks and nymphs of the pave, was still doing her stuff :

"P.C. William Jones said that about half past nine o'clock on Thursday night Anne Awberry was drunk in Guildhall Square. She had a crowd of children about her and was singing and dancing and very riotous. She is a prostitute. She was committed to the House of Correction for two months." (C.J.)

*　　　*　　　*

"P.C. David James charged Anne Awberry with being drunk and riotous. He said ' Last night about eleven o'clock I was on duty in Lammas Street when I saw defendant there near the Boar's Head Hotel. She was singing and making a great noise. She was very drunk and creating a disturbance. She has been very bad since she came out of gaol last. She is a prostitute and

"... on the fashionable parade" (1874)

Guildhall Square in 1861. The steps were removed in the following year

The Joint Counties Lunatic Asylum (now Saint David's Mental Hospital), opened
in November 1865

Carmarthen Infirmary, Priory Street, opened on 1st July, 1858

Carmarthen, 1865

this is her *hundred and thirtieth appearance here.*' Committed
to the House of Correction for three calendar months."
(C.J.)

*   *   *

So celebrated was "Poor Nanny" that she earned a distinction unique for one of the "lower orders" in those days—an
obituary in the *Carmarthen Journal* :

> "*Death of 'Poor Nanny'* : This notorious person known
> as Anne Awberry is no more. She was only lately dis-
> charged from gaol where ' Poor Nanny ' as she called
> herself had spent most part of her time for the last
> thirty years, as an incorrigible drunkard. She was taken
> suddenly ill on Thursday and conveyed in a cart to the
> Workhouse, where medical assistance was given her,
> but of no avail, and she died on Sunday last (the 23rd of
> August, 1863)." (C.J.)

Sad that only this kind of notoriety could merit even a
mention of the passing of those below the rank of "gentleman",
professional man or tradesman ; only an entry in a court
record or a police occurrence book would mark their brief transit
across Carmarthen's crowded little stage. Others of the "lower
orders" entered and left that stage without leaving even a foot-
print on its boards.

BROKEN LINKS

The 1860s saw the passing of three other Carmarthen characters whose going represented, in different ways, the end of an
era.

At his large residence on the fashionable Parade, Captain
John George Philipps, R.N., breathed his last on Saturday the
24th of April, 1869—at the age of eighty-five. The fiery old
dragon of the 1831 election riots who, as the first Mayor of the
reformed borough, got his revenge by sacking Lazenby, who
had locked up his supporters in those riots, was gone. He was
born in 1783 when Pitt the Younger became Prime Minister,
when the great Napoleon was still at Brienne Cadet School in

France, an unknowing fellow cadet (it is said) of the author of his final eclipse—Arthur Wellesley, the first Duke of Wellington—and six years before George Washington became the first President of the United States of America. As a midshipman of fifteen he had seen Nelson sweep the French fleet from the waters of Alexandria, before the first steamship had taken to the water, and when the journey over the rough tracks from oil-lit Carmarthen to London took nearly a week by coach. And now, within sight of the busy railway line which had brought the town to within six and a half hours of the Capital, and within sound of the whistles of the steamships coming up to Carmarthen Quay bringing mass produced wares to a prosperous middle-class that had not existed when he was a boy, old John George Philipps said farewell to a world that had left him far behind.

Perhaps the electric telegraph (which had not existed when it took a month for the news of the Battle of the Nile to reach his home town) conveyed news of the Captain's death to Brecon in time for the next edition of the local weekly paper. John Lazenby would have read it with memories of the events of thirty-three years ago—for he was still there, as Governor of Brecon Gaol, and he would survive the old Captain by more than twenty years yet !

Irishman Nicholas Martin, indefatigable founder-member of Carmarthen's "New" police force and one of the first to be appointed by John George Philipps and his Watch Committee, salvor of the force's tattered reputation in Rebecca's Talog ambush, and holder of the all-time record of (at least) forty-four disciplinary convictions, *was still patrolling the streets of Carmarthen in 1861 at the age of sixty-seven.* Still locking them up, still unable to write his own reports in the books, still giving evidence in court. And in the classic style of the proverbial "Old Soldier" he simply "faded away" ; simply dropped out of the records leaving a question only answered by a visit to Saint Mary's Roman Catholic Churchyard. There, by the Church door, stands a headstone bearing the inscription "In Memory of Nicholas Martin, who died 30th November, 1861, aged 67. He was for 26 years a member of the Police Force for this Borough. May he Rest in Peace."

And on the 31st of August, 1866, the *Carmarthen Journal* recorded the death of the last survivor of the old "Watch"— the last link with old Wil y Lôn, the last of those who, muffled and cloaked, carrying their flickering lanterns like glow-worms in the dark, had broken the silence of the night with the comforting cry "Starlight, fair, and all's well".

> "Death of an Old Inhabitant : Our obituary this week records the death of an aged and somewhat remarkable inhabitant of this Town, Mr. David Woozley. The deceased was in his youth a member of the old County Militia and accompanied his Corps to Ireland.[19] Before the days of policemen he was enrolled in the ranks of those Guardians of the Public Peace scarcely less ancient than night itself—*The watchmen.*
>
> Most of our readers have had the satisfaction of listening to the strains of what was known as the Carmarthen Old Band, the members of which never failed to turn out and do their best towards enlivening the town on all notable public occasions. Those who have not heard them will never have that pleasure in this world, for old David Woozley was the last but one of the company who have, let us hope, been made members of another and better band.
>
> Late in life Mr. Woozley was appointed as keeper of the station house, which office he held for thirty-three years, and up to the day of his death giving entire satisfaction to the public.[20] He was of great height and was *eighty-two years old* when he died.
>
> Many members of the police force attended as pallbearers at the funeral, which was perhaps the largest and most respectable of its kind ever witnessed in Carmarthen." (C.J.)

Old Wil y Lôn would never have had such a send-off. Truly, Carmarthen had come a long way.

NOTES

[1]Carmarthen fitted perfectly the prescription for a cholera epidemic : "Attacks of cholera are found uniformly to be most frequent and virulent in low-lying districts, on the banks of rivers in the neighbourhood of sewer mouths, and wherever there are large collections of refuse, particularly amidst human dwellings. Abominations meet the eye of those who visit the courts, alleys and passages in various parts of the town. We find that the houses in one of the chief entrances to the town, Priory Street, have drains running through them, which together with a pig-sty here and there empty their contents into the public streets." (*Carmarthen Journal*)

[2]For which read "English and Welsh", the distinction between them being of comparatively modern usage (see, for example, Edward C. Lloyd Hall's reference to Carmarthenshire "and the rest of England", Chapter 5, page 65)

[3]A phenomenal and even frightening speed for those who had never seen a railway engine before—that is all but a handful of the townspeople. The horse had provided the fastest motive power in their experience.

[4] & [5]*Carmarthen Journal.*

[6]"Hordes" of starving Irish peasants walked into Carmarthen during the potato famine years of 1845-50 as they were landed by the ship load along the south west coast of Wales. They were given a meal at the workhouse and escorted out of town by the police, but many returned under cover of darkness. They settled in the crowded riverside area. At least one of those immigrant families provided a Mayor for the town in a later generation. Tom Hurley was Town Mayor in 1975/76. His ancestors were in Kidwelly Fach in 1848.

[7]Named after the Quaker Joseph Lancaster (1778-1838) who devised a school system based on ' Monitors '—senior pupils who passed on their knowledge to their juniors under the supervision of teachers who were thus able to supervise as many as a hundred pupils each.

[8]All coracle families of very ancient origin, whose descendants ply the river in their little craft to this day.

[9]Dyfed County Record Office—Museum Collection.

[10]A Cwrw Bach (lit. "Small Beer") was an unlicensed drinking party where a householder sold beer at prices even less than those in the pubs. It was commonly a form of wedding party among the "lower orders".

[11]Still open for business on the corner of Lammas Street and Water Street.

[12]Nancy Black Cap.

[13]At Alltycnap, out beyond Johnstown near the western boundary of the Borough.

[14]A "Bidding" was the means of poorer couples obtaining goods and money with which to set up their first home on marriage. The word went around, or an advertisement was put abroad by poster or newspaper notice, that a wedding was to take place. All who came with presents were entertained with food and drink, and could be assured that the young couple would respond in kind to any future "Bidding" advertised by any of their guests.

[15]To the officers and men of the 23rd Regiment, Royal Welsh Fusiliers, killed in the Crimean war (see page 336).

[16]The Carmarthen historian.

[17]A future Chief Constable of the Borough !

[18]Only as a last resort were "Gentlemen" handled in the same way as the "lower orders" ; a deferential attitude comes over very strongly from the records.

[19]In 1801/1802, while that country was still in the throes of rebellion.

[20]He was succeeded as station house keeper by Sergeant David Williams.

CHAPTER EIGHT

THE EBBING TIDE

IF there were signs that Carmarthen was shedding its old violent image and that most of its people were coming to terms with the police as a brake on their more boisterous behaviour and as protectors rather than oppressors, there were other developments at this time that were of equally fundamental significance for the future character of the town.

The 1860s saw a quickening of the changes in the lives of the men of the Towy—the coraclemen, the Seine-netters, the sailors, shippers, merchants and quay hobblers. The ebbing tide of their way of life began to flow that little bit faster, hastening the time when the town would finally turn its back on a river bereft of shipping and lined by dereliction and neglect.

One day in 1938, another of those quiet moments of history would touch the old town as a dirty, tall-funnelled old 250-ton coal burner that had delivered a cargo of flour from Bristol would be untied from bollards worn by countless ropes over countless years, above the steps by the old Jolly Tar pub. History would whisper to the few watchers on the quay as she puffed away down the broad, winding river to the sea . . . leaving Carmarthen a port no more.

The tide was also ebbing for a group of men whose first entry into the story of Carmarthen was made at a point almost beyond the reach of history and who were once almost as much a part of the river Towy as the very water itself. It would ebb to a time in the second half of the twentieth century when the river would be virtually deserted by its fishermen and when a three-lane highway would wipe out all trace of their habitations, separate the town from its river, and be called—with supreme and apparently unconscious irony—*Coracle Way*.

The coraclemen of Carmarthen, who can lay just claim to an unbroken line of descent from the town's earliest inhabitants, have been met many times in this story and have already left their distinctive stamp on it : their prominence in food and election riots, their rowdy support for Rebecca and their violent feuding with their Seine-netting Ferryside rivals, their regular court appearances over domestic squabbles and battles with the town's police. But all this can too easily obscure another side of their contribution to the story of Carmarthen . . . their perpetuation of ancient skills and crafts, their equally ancient tradition of unwritten laws, and their transition from the "lower orders"—with all that that term connotes in poverty, hardship and distress—to the kind of small elite they are to-day : the survivors of a hardy race.

A hardy race indeed, for despite the privations of their way of life they provided notable exceptions to Carmarthen's notoriously high death-rate,[1] as was demonstrated in January, 1887, when a townsman wrote of the death of David Elias "at the ripe old age of ninety-one" :

> "I have noticed the longevity of the fishermen generally. For instance T. Lewis died when he was 88 years of age, J. Elias when he was 92, T. Evans at 80, D. Evans at 82, Owen Elias at 81, J. Lewis at 84, D. Edwards at 91, William Evans at 85, Griffith Lewis at 80, William Richards at 75, David Samuels at 75, Thomas Richards at 72, and many others at ages ranging from 79 to 90. There are a few now alive and attending their Chapel regularly who are over 80 years of age. It will be found that the fishermen are living to a ripe old age and are all very healthy even in their last days." (C.J.)

Hard drinking, hard fighting, a subsistence diet and exposure to the cold, damp air of nights on the water would hardly be thought of as the classical ingredients of a long and healthy life! But as if to press the point, the *Carmarthen Journal* reported in March, 1892, on—

> "*A drunken octogenarian pauper* : At the Borough Police Court, Daniel Jones, coracleman, an indoor pauper, was summoned for being helplessly drunk in the borough. The defendant said he had been in the Workhouse throughout the winter. On the Saturday in question he

met a few friends in Priory Street (where a number of the coraclemen lived) and was treated to some beer. He was born in 1806, being consequently 86 years of age. The old man, who appeared hale and hearty, begged the Bench to overlook the offence, which they did, and he was discharged." (C.J.)

The Lewises, the Thomases, the Eliases, the Owens and the Evanses are still coracle fishing and their families were probably in Carmarthen before the Romans came. Certainly Giraldus Cambrensis saw their little craft on the river eight hundred years ago ". . . made of twigs, not oblong nor pointed, but almost round, or rather triangular, covered both within and without with raw hides." And coracles were referred to as far back as five hundred years before that.

Back before the dawn of Christianity they go, to ancestors who, they say, placated the river Gods by the ritual burning of their worn-out coracles. To this day—despite the introduction of nylon nets, fibreglass coracles and other examples of twentieth century technology—the descendants of those whom Giraldus Cambrensis described have the skills of their forefathers in plaiting the ash and willow frames and fitting the tarred calico skins of the coracles, of weaving cows' and horses' tails into ropes and cutting cows' horns into rings for the running lines of the nets held between the pairs of coracles—skills handed down from time immemorial. At least one present-day coracle-man[2] casts his lead net-weights in a mould used by his great-great-grandfather (one of the Eliases) in a manner taught him by his ninety-year-old grandfather, who also taught him the medieval Welsh terms that are part of the coracle tradition.

Walking along the riverside of a still evening, before the incoming tide begins to cover the shingle banks, you might chance to sense the sweet smell of hot tar and to see smoke rising lazily into the air, up beyond the town bridge, as a much-patched and worn-out coracle burns its own brand of incense. To the river Gods ? Only the coracle men know that. And they are not known for telling their secrets.

A TURBULENT RACE

When Wil y Lôn walked the dark streets of Carmarthen and George the Third reigned, as the eighteenth century gave way to the nineteenth, *four hundred coracles* fished the Towy, to give a precarious and irregular living for nearly a third of the town's inhabitants. The coraclemen shared the river with the sailing ships and with the little boats shuttling between Carmarthen and Ferryside at the river mouth . . . but they shared it with no one else. Woe betide anyone who encroached on their private domain. Nearly two-thirds of the way through the nineteenth century it could still be said of them that—

> "The coraclemen are a turbulent race, setting the law at defiance and ready to take it into their own hands. They encroach on private property, they appropriate the public water by attacking and driving from it other men whose interests they deem hostile to their own.
>
> On more than one occasion they have made the use of Seine-nets below an occasion for riot, and last July (1864) eleven of them were convicted for forcibly seizing and destroying one of those nets." (C.J.)

The violent feud with the Ferrysiders over where the boundary line should lie between Seine and coracle-netting had persisted for centuries and is still spoken of from first-hand experience by the old men of the coracle families. The incident referred to here happened on the 15th of June, 1864, between eight and nine o'clock in the evening, when Mr. Robert Parnall of Llanstephan, his friends Mr. James and Mr. Davies, and two of his employees, John David and John Jones, were Seine-netting on the Ferryside side of the river between Pilroath and Pilglas down near the estuary. They had a small boat in which they had placed their catch of three sewin and two bass, and they were hauling in the net for the fourth time when they saw a flotilla of coracles bearing down on them. Before they knew where they were ten of the coracles were upon them. Their occupants leapt out wielding paddles and "knock-sticks"[3] with which they belaboured the Seine-netters unmercifully, shouting "We've caught the buggers. Smash the boat."

While the ten were engaged with the Llanstephan men, the eleventh coracleman—one legged William Owen—caught up with them and grabbed the net, which he and others tore into shreds. It was to no avail that Parnall and his friends insisted that the net was of the legal mesh, because the coraclemen said they would rather be transported[4] than allow anyone to fish with Seine-nets, even in the estuary.

During the course of the riot—for that was the offence with which they were later to be charged—they asked for the whereabouts of another Seine-netter nicknamed "Carew". Fortunately for "Carew" he was nowhere about ; they said they would have broken his arms if they could have found him !

A fortnight later the coraclemen were before the magistrates. One-legged William Owen of Bridge Street, John Lewis of Dan y Banc, David Lewis of Towyside, William Lewis of Dan y Banc, John Lewis who lived on the Quay, John Edwards of Old Priory, John Lewis of Priory Street, John Davies of Dame Street and David Lewis of Kidwelly Fach, were charged with destroying the net, with assault and with riotous assembly. As ever, there was uproar in court, not only from the defendants but also from a gallery full of relatives and fellow fishermen, and the police were hotly engaged in restoring order.

They were all committed for trial at the Quarter Sessions, where they were convicted only on the charge of destroying the net, for which each of them was sentenced to a week's hard labour in Carmarthen Gaol. "Hard Labour" meant many weary hours trudging on the treadwheel, by means of which the gaol's water supply was pumped. Presumably some other form of hard labour was found for one-legged Billy Owen !

Another incident of this kind gave rise to the tradition of the "Battle of Banc yr Alma" and the creation of the "Yankee" branch of one of the coracle families. The crossing of the Alma river under fire and the storming by the British infantry of the Russian entrenchments on top of the Alma heights in 1854, one of the most stirring of the Crimean victories, must have been still fresh in people's minds[5] when the coracle fishers and the Seine-netters (women as well as men) met at low water on a river sandbank, and it is hardly surprising that the sandbank, opposite Siggery's Cottage halfway down river should thereafter be called Banc yr Alma. Blood had already been shed and bones had already been broken before a loud report and the collapse of a Ferryside woman with shotgun wounds sent people scattering in all directions. It is said that one of the coraclemen did not stop running until he reached America where he married and raised a family, never knowing that the injured woman had lived. Years later some of his descendants returned to Carmarthen to found a branch of the family known to this day as the "Yankees". So legend has it.

Despite the occasional eruption of internecine warfare and family disputes, the coraclemen formed a tightly-knit brotherhood ruled by unwritten but well understood and ruthlessly enforced laws. Old Bill Evans remembers vividly being called upon as a boy to help his father drive off the river a pair of coracles whose occupants had had the temerity to enter the water before the tide had properly turned and before darkness had fallen sufficiently, thus gaining an advantage over those who would observe the rules. They did it by hurling stones at them in an attempt to sink them !

Even their language—a relic of the medieval Welsh—added to the "Secret Society" flavour of their relationship, and the outsider could glean nothing of their intentions, of their intimate knowledge of the river, or of the size of their catches. And there were good reasons for their fierce siege mentality. Sitting on the knife-edge between subsistence and starvation, packed into tiny, insanitary riverside hovels, illiterate, improvident and drunken, they were fighting for survival. Early in the nineteenth century they could be found at the head of any mob of starving wretches smashing their way into food stores ; they ransacked the cheese ships in 1818 and stood their ground in the front ranks of the rioters when the Yeomanry Cavalry, sabres drawn, clattered along the quay ; they vented their frustrations and wilder natures in the violence of elections from which the likes of them were otherwise excluded.

But it was not all violence. Their boisterousness found an equally ready outlet in those events which brought out all the wilder side of the Carmarthen nature, from all classes of the townspeople—Christmas Eve's "Torch-night", the burning of Ceffylau Pren, Royal marriages and birthdays, victory celebrations, river regattas (of which the coracle races were always a highlight), race days and fair days.

There was a great capacity for enjoyment among the "lower orders", for all that they had to endure, and we must remind ourselves that we are in errror if we impute to them the social and economic aspirations of the late twentieth century. The common portrayal of unhappy wretches living lives of unrelieved gloom and despair owes much to twentieth-century hindsight.

A FORLORN PREDICAMENT

For centuries, then, the fishermen had lived in their close-knit community and their use of the river had gone virtually unchallenged, so the impact on their way of life of the first determined attempt by Parliament to regulate their activities can well be imagined.

In 1861 the Government set up a commission on salmon fishery to conduct an investigation into every aspect of estuarial and river fishery conservation, and Parliament passed a Salmon Fisheries Act prescribing seasons, regulating methods, defining fishing areas and—most provocative of all to the coraclemen—issuing licences. To men dependent on the fishing for their livelihood and accustomed to virtually total freedom on the river, the licensing of coracles threatened extinction.

The new law was resisted, by subterfuge and even by physical violence, and given the severity of the courts towards the "lower orders" in the mid-nineteenth century, the leniency of the Carmarthen magistrates in fishery cases is surprising. Or is it ? There were those in and around the town who were uncharitable enough to impute selfish motives to some of Their Worships, and there was even an application to the High Court in London for an order compelling certain of them to convict in a case they had dismissed. The order was sought on the grounds that the bench had been composed of magistrates who were themselves regular purchasers of fish poached by the coraclemen, but the application was dismissed for lack of evidence—*even though it was accepted that one of those dealing with the disputed case had purchased the actual salmon in question from the defendant* !

The 1865 report of the Inspector of Salmon Fisheries uttered a veritable *cri de coeur* on this very point, with the observation that—

> "The poaching in and about Carmarthen is a serious evil. The poachers all start from the town, return there, bring their fish and sell them publicly there, in season and out, clean or foul, and there have not been two convictions for the last ten years."

But physical violence towards the water bailiffs was an altogether different matter, and some murderous assaults were committed. Whereas the traditional picture is of the poacher on the defensive against the bailiffs, the situation on the Towy, where the coraclemen were well known for their aggressive nature, was quite the opposite, as poor William Palmer found one moonlit night in June, 1868 when he saw eight coracles coming up the river towards the town :

> "Five of them landed close to where he was and he went up the embankment into the field. Five of the men came after him, the two defendants Griffith Lewis and Thomas Elias being the foremost. They struck at him with the oars of their coracles, inflicting injury to his hand. They beat him all over the body, so badly that he was obliged to be examined by a surgeon and was confined to his house for a fortnight. He was insensible after the first two blows. They thought they had killed him he was sure." (C. J.)

The defence was alibi—they were somewhere else at the time —and who else but a fellow coracleman to look the magistrates straight in the eye and without a blush support that alibi :

> "William Thomas swore that on the 28th of June the two defendants were in his company from 8 p.m. to 11 p.m. at the 'Ship' public house in Blue Street. When he left them they were very drunk." (C.J.)

The magistrates found no difficulty in disbelieving "Curly" Thomas, and they sent Lewis and Elias to prison for a month— with hard labour.

But Carmarthen would not have been Carmarthen if they had merely gone quietly off to gaol. Oh, no :

> "On the removal of the men to gaol, a large crowd of fishermen and others assembled and an attempt was made to assault some of the magistrates. The police were rather roughly handled, but they succeeded in handing over the defendants to the custody of the gaol authorities." (C.J.)

Even in the eighties and nineties, and beyond the turn of the century, some of the coraclemen clung violently to their heritage, as in 1887, when—

> "William Owens, David Richards, Joseph Bowen, John Lewis and John Owens were charged with being in possession of unclean salmon, and the Bench fined them £5 each[6] or in default one month's imprisonment. The defendants announced their intention of ' going in ' (instead of paying their fines), but their conduct in the courtroom was so unruly that the police were obliged to turn them out. When outside, the defendants seem to have caught sight of the fish (four fine large salmon) in the possession of the water bailiffs, and desire seized them to become possessed of that which had cost them so dear. Accordingly, one of the Owens made a dash at the fish, followed by the other two, assisted by a large crowd of men and women, the latter kicking up a nice hullaballoo.
>
> The bailiffs drew their staves and let fly, and it is said that John Lewis received a crack on the head— which helped him to forget for the moment the mortification of his conviction and fine. At about this time the police interfered and the bailiffs got home with their fish." (C.J.)

For this, the coraclemen were later fined another five shillings (25p) each.

Yes, the coraclemen fought long and hard, but the writing loomed large upon the wall, and within a few years the inevitable happened. The coracle "fleet" was decimated, the remaining fishermen were licensed, and those displaced had found other occupations, some by emigration. And so it continued steadily to the 1930s from when the size of the coracle "fleet" levelled out at the dozen pairs we know to-day.

The turbulent traditions of the men of the Towy were, of course, eroded by a number of other influences, notably the temperance movement of the eighties and nineties and the great Welsh religious revival of the beginning of the twentieth century, which achieved something particularly remarkable. Under their influence several of the coraclemen became tee-totallers !

Of more long-term significance, though, was the fact that the children of the riverside were undergoing compulsory education in the Blue Street, Bridge Street, Towyside and Priory Street elementary schools, and being influenced by the moral teachings of the church and chapel Sunday Schools, to which they flocked in their "Sunday Best". The rising generation was being given a key to a door marked "Exit"—a door leading out of the "forlorn predicament of relying upon the coracle net alone for sustenance", which had largely dictated the old way of life of the Carmarthen coracle families.

"I was called to Dan y Banc"

But back to the years of struggle, which would be lost to all but family tradition, fisheries reports and newspaper court reports if it were not for the unique record of some aspects of the daily life of the coracle families preserved in the few surviving police occurrence books.

It is many years now—a couple of generations or more—since the coraclemen ceased to figure on the books of the "Carmarthen Shilling" and to provide them with so much of their daily work, but since even a century is not a long time among a people still noted for their longevity, a little anonymity here and there might not go amiss. So with that in mind, we take a few glimpses of life on the riverside in the later years of the nineteenth century :

"Monday 17th July, 1876. A row near the Bridge. Sergeant Lewis Hughes reports—I was called to Bridge Street by a woman named Evans, alias 'Ball Court','

No. 2 Bridge Street, who said that her brother was nearly killed by John . . ., fisherman, Dan y Banc. I went there and saw a large crowd of women and a few fishermen. I saw John . . ., who complained to me that he could not have quiet to walk the street with the ' Ball Courts ' and that he had been assaulted by them. There was no fighting or assaults committed while I was there, but the women were very noisy. P.C. Jones No. 8 and Dunleavy No. 6 were also there and while we were near Bridge Street two or three women were in Guildhall Square, Nott Square and King Street shouting ' Murder near the Bridge '. They disturbed the whole street. We cleared the streets and saw all quiet."

*　　*　　*

"Saturday 11th August, 1877. About 11.30 p.m. I was on duty in King Street by the corner of Queen Street when I heard a woman shouting out ' Murder '. I ran down towards Bridge Street when I was informed of a row on the Quay by the Bridge. I at once went down there, saw Henry . . ., son of William . . ., fisherman, and John . . ., Dan y Banc, fisherman, fighting. I separated them and told Henry . . . to go home, which he did. At the time, Margaret Evans, Bridge Street, alias ' Ball Court ', rushed on and struck Martha . . ., wife of William . . ., about the head two or three times. I told her to go home. She was very noisy, cursing and swearing and some of the crowd took her home. I then turned back and saw David . . ., labourer, Quay. He was drunk and very noisy, cursing and swearing. I requested him to go home, he refused. I then took hold of him, when his mother and some others beg on me to let them take him to the house. I then gave him up to them, when he became very abusive and kicking. They had to take off his boots and carry him to the house. I saw him in. P.C. Evan Evans, No.3."

*　　*　　*

135

The coraclemen were often involved in the search for bodies in the river. One way or another, through bathing accidents, falls from the quay and from ships, and through suicides, a number of people drowned each year and, having no equipment of their own, the police would call on the coraclemen, who would know exactly where to look. There was the incentive of the Coroner's fee for the recovery of a body. Old Bill Evans remembers that it was higher in the county than in the borough —twelve shillings and sixpence (62½p) as against seven shillings and six-pence (37½p).

He also remembers that as often as they could, he and the others used to push the bodies to the Pensarn bank so that they qualified for the higher fee !

Griffith and John Lewis (father and son) were well into the county and the higher rate when they picked up the body of one of the town's prostitutes from Cook's Bank,[8] 2½ miles down river one morning in July, 1891. She had met her end the night before while plying her trade below the Quay :

> "On Wednesday night about 9.20, Kate Bear (alias
> ' Beelzebub '), an Unfortunate,[9] was drowned in the
> Towy. It appears that at the time mentioned she was
> going with her paramour on board a little German
> vessel 'Alpha', which was anchored opposite the saw-
> mills, and when halfway over the plank leading on deck
> she overbalanced herself and fell into the river, the
> current at the time being very strong. Yesterday morn-
> ing, Griffith and John Lewis were out coracle fishing
> and found the body on Cook's Bank. The body was
> brought up in a boat and landed at the Pothouse at ten
> to six a.m. P.C. Thomas Davies procured a stretcher
> and the woman was conveyed to her house in Mill
> Street." (C.J.)

*   *   *

> "Saturday 3rd July, 1880. Sergeant David Williams
> reports that about 12 noon this day he received infor-
> mation from Benjamin, son of William Lewis, Dan y
> Banc, fisherman, that the house of William Thomas,

". . . the little boats shuttling between Carmarthen and Ferryside" (1874)

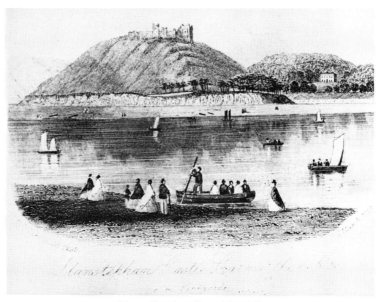

Llansteffan, from Ferryside, 1865

FISHERMEN WITH CORACLES

Coraclemen in the 1850s

" . . . a hardy race"—Coraclemen in the 1890s. Left to right: Dai Lewis, Spring Gardens; Dai 'Bigan' Thomas, Priory Street; 'Billy Boy' Owens; Jack Williams, 40 Mill Street; Griffith Lewis, Towyside; Harry 'Ship' Evans (of the branch of the family who kept the Ship Inn, Blue Street)

Carmarthen Coraclemen in the 1890s

Steam Mill, fisherman, was on fire. He went at once to the spot and found the premises full of smoke, a number of fishermen and others engaged in carrying water and throwing it about the upper lofts which were the part occupied by William Thomas. The reel and hose were taken there in a very short time. Mr. Superintendent James and P.Cs. No. 4, 6, 7 and 9 came there. From enquiries made it appears that William Thomas was in a room making a fishing net when Henry his eldest son was engaged in melting and boiling some pitch and tar in an iron kettle[10] while his two sisters, named Margaret aged 14 and Susan aged 12 were in the same room. While Henry was in the act of taking the kettle off the fire some of the contents spilled on the fire and blazed, burning his arm. He then threw the kettle over the stairs, which went in a blaze. He cried out to his father and also to a younger brother named Stephen. Both came down over the stairs but were severely burned, and both were taken to the infirmary.[11]

Margaret was taken out through a window and over a ladder by Griffith Lewis, fisherman, and Susan was taken down the same way by Phillip Baskerville, a man in the employ of the Telegraph Company. The windows were forced and broken open to allow the smoke to go out. The damage from the fire and water was a good deal and the premises are not insured."

* * *

"Sunday 4th September, 1881. P.C. Thomas Davies No. 4[12] reports that he patrolled King Street centre beat (part) and saw the following public houses open : King's Head, Bridge Street, kept by Rachel Davies at 12.35 p.m. Also Pelican in the same street, kept by David Davies. Also the Boat, Priory Street, kept by David Evans. Also the Railway Inn kept by Jonathan Hodges open about 1 p.m. and the following parties drinking on the premises—John Lewis, Sawyer's Arms, Priory Street, fisherman ; John Lewis Jnr. alias 'Bryncelli',

fisherman ; Frederick Elias, Dan y Banc, fisherman ;
Owen Elias, Dan y Banc, labourer and fisherman ;
James Tought, Tin Works, labourer ; David Rees, Mill
Street, fitter ; Tom Jones, of the Parade."[13]

*   *   *

"29th March, 1881. P.C. Jonathan Arthur No. 7
reports that about 7.25 he saw Sarah . . ., alias ' Sally
Piss ', Morfa, wife of William . . ., labourer and coracleman, Quay, in a boat very drunk and threatening to
throw herself in the river, the tide going out strong at the
time. With assistance of two men he got her out and
took her to her house and saw her in charge of her
husband, who was sober. Said that he would not have
her go out again."

*   *   *

"Saturday night 30th June, 1881. P.C. Thomas Davies
No. 4 reports that about 9.45 p.m. he was called to Dan
y Banc. Went there and saw a crowd and William . . .,
fisherman, of Dan y Banc, with his coat off and wanting
to fight Frederick . . . and David . . ., fishermen of
the same place. He requested them to go away, which
they did. He dispersed the crowd and saw all quiet.
The parties had been drinking but were not drunk."

*   *   *

"Monday 2nd January, 1882. P.C. Thomas Rees
No. 9 reports that at 3.30 p.m. he found by the Golden
Anchor, corner of Queen Street, the footway crowded by
some women. They all went away except Martha, wife
of William . . ., Steam Mill. Then he went away and
she became very noisy, swearing and shouting at the top
of her voice causing a crowd to collect in the street.
He went back to her and requested her to go away
quiet and in reply she swore at him and said ' I will not

go to please the Devil.' He then took her in custody and she became very violent towards him by kicking, beating and biting and resisted very much. While so doing the following parties pulled and rescued her from custody—Jane, wife of William . . ., Dan y Banc, Catherine, wife of Thomas . . . of the same place, Elizabeth, wife of John . . ., Priory Street, fisherman, William . . ., labourer of Spilman Street, and Joseph . . ., of Quay, fisherman. The latter also assaulted him. They were all drunk."

*　　*　　*

"Saturday 11th February, 1882. P.C. Thomas Rees No. 9 reports that about 7.50 p.m. he was on duty in Guildhall Square when Elizabeth, wife of Frederick . . . labourer and fisherman, Kidwelly Fach, said to him 'I want you to lock me up as I have in a basket an un-season salmon which I caught myself with a net in the River Towy'. She walk with him to the station house and he took possession of it and it is now in the police station."

*　　*　　*

"Saturday 4th March, 1882. P.C. William Thomas No. 6 reports that P.C. David Davies, No. 17, County Police, stationed at Llandysul, complained to him that about 10 p.m. he was conveying a prisoner from the town railway station to Gaol and on top of the steps there was a crowd, and one of them took his coat off and struck him as he was trying to pass. Some man who was passing by at the time told him it was Thomas . . ., son of William . . ., alias ' . . .', fisherman. He was drunk."

NOTES

[1] In 1873, Carmarthen had the highest annual death-rate in the Kingdom—31.68 per thousand, as compared with the national average of only 22.4. In the rural areas the average age at death was 39 years ; in the town it was only 33, while in England and Wales as a whole it was 41. Only one in six died of old age in Carmarthen town !

[2] Raymond Rees, an acknowledged authority on the coracle tradition and himself an active coracle maker and fisher.

[3] "Cnocer" in Welsh ; the club used to stun the fish.

[4] Co-incidentally, the year 1864 was the year when transportation to Australia or Tasmania ceased to be used as a punishment for crime.

[5] A man from Friar's Park, Carmarthen, a private in the 23rd Regiment, the Royal Welsh Fusiliers, was the first British soldier killed in this, the first battle of the Crimean campaign, hence, it is said, the choice of Carmarthen for the Regiment's monument, which stands at the junction of Lammas Street with Water Street.

[6] This represented some 63lbs. weight of fish, at retail prices, making their loss considerably greater.

[7] The nickname ' Ball Court ' had attached to the Evanses since at least 1819, the most prominent of them being one of the 1831 election rioters and later one of the founder-members of the borough police force. The foundations of No. 2 Bridge Street now lie under the three-lane highway called "Coracle Way".

[8] The stone for building the "Lunatic Asylum" (now St. David's Mental Hospital) in 1863/65 was quarried at Green Castle and brought up river on barges. If caught on the ebbing tide the men camped and cooked their meals on this bank while waiting for water to float off. Hence "Cooks Bank".

[9] A euphemism for "Prostitute".

[10] For coating the calico covering of a coracle.

[11] William Thomas's wife, Martha, was thrown out of the Infirmary the next night—for being drunk and riotous !

[12] A farm servant from Llanarthne : joined August 1878 ; promoted Sergeant October 1902 ; retired on pension May, 1911.

[13] Sunday was *dry* in Carmarthen !

CHAPTER NINE

"THE TOWN CLOCK DON'T STRICK ALL NIGHT"

"Wednesday 7th September, 1870. Night fine. Moonlight. Nothing to report during the night, all being very quiet. Lodging houses visited.
The Town Clock don't strick all night."

*   *   *

So wrote Constable No. 2 William Jones in his slow but beautiful copperplate hand in the night report book as he, Sergeant David Williams and the other night men brought their shift to an end at six in the morning in the old Cambrian Place station house.

A quiet night in Carmarthen ? It is a measure of how far the town had come from the "nightly riots and depredations" and the military interventions of less than thirty years before, that by the seventies such a report as this no longer raised any eyebrows. But it was still something of a rarity ; more often there were equally brief entries accounting for rather livelier nights, entries like—

"The P.Cs. reports that there was several rows and fights during the night and they prevented many fights and disturbances in Blue Street and Dame Street. Much complaints made. Lodging houses visited. A cloudy night—small rain. David Williams, Sergeant."

and

"The steamer discharged on the quay this night. Several rows about the streets this night. Lodging houses visited. Fine weather. Lewis Hughes, Sergeant."[1]

But the "Carmarthen Shilling" was firmly in control, respected or feared as the occasion demanded and as much a part of the social scene as any other institution—in contrast to the struggle against the general antipathy that accompanied the creation of the "new police" thirty-five years before. Over the last twenty-two of those years Chief Constable Samuel Kentish had brought a previously unknown stability to the force. Although his men were still hard drinkers, with the inevitable disciplinary consequences, they served for longer and longer as the force found that vital *esprit de corps* which only good and strong leadership can create. This could not be bad in a tiny force that had seen the comings and goings of well over a hundred men *in only thirty-four years*, and especially when most of the "goings" had the smell of drink about them ![2]

They even looked more like modern policemen, the top hat, tail coat and white "duck" trousers having been foresaken in recent years in favour of helmet, long, belted, through-buttoned tunic, and cape.

In December, 1870, Samuel Kentish retired on pension— after 22 years—and for the remaining eight years of his life he remained in Carmarthen. For the next five years the force was led by a member of an old Carmarthen family, Captain D.I. Brown-Edwardes of Rhydygors, a Militia officer with no police background, but with an experience of military command and discipline which was a highly regarded quality for a Chief Constable, even well into the twentieth century. His successor was Frank D. Lewis, who resigned after only ten months.

By August, 1877, the force was back in the hands of a professional policeman, chosen from a short-list of sixteen policemen and army officers. George James, ex-Glamorganshire Police Sergeant and now Chief Warder of Carmarthenshire County Gaol, had a quality which was bound to appeal to the Watch Committee. Alderman Rowlands said he was—

> " . . . the most soberest of men that could possibly be, and unfortunately the opposite quality was a national evil among us and very rife in the town of Carmarthen. It was an evil which had damaged several of their former officers. Mr. James was wholly free from that, and he believed it was no small advantage to have a man for the office of Chief Constable who was a teetotaller !" (C.J.)

George James served the borough for ten years, until his

death in 1887, when he was succeeded by the man who would take the "Carmarthen Shilling" into the twentieth century. Big, brown-bearded Thomas Smith had served for sixteen years with the Swansea force and was a Detective Sergeant with a reputation earned on a hard, dockland beat when he answered Carmarthen's advertisement for a Chief Constable. By the time he retired on pension at the end of 1911 he had been a policeman for forty years. He died in 1933 at the age of eighty-two.

And what of the town he came to ?

The last thirty years of the 19th century which saw the changes that foreshadowed the end of the River Towy as a force in the economy of Carmarthen were also to see the last of the town's principal industries—weaving, iron and tin—decline to the point of extinction. That century would then have seen Carmarthen succumb to the challenge of the industrial revolution, to decline in status from the most populous and important town in Wales and the principal seaport of the south west of the Principality to an agricultural town of small, virtually static, population.

This decline in status and fortune brought with it many social problems, including unemployment, works closures and an exacerbation of the twin Carmarthen curses of poverty and drink, and of the seemingly insuperable health, sanitation and water-supply problems posed by the decay of the older and poorer sections of the town. Even so, Carmarthen was still an important and largely prosperous market town for a richly agricultural county, an asset which, in spite of all, guaranteed a stable future in a fast-changing world. But before that stable future was reached, a good many people in the town would continue to experience much poverty and distress and the crowded soup kitchen for the poor would be a feature of the Carmarthen winter scene well beyond the century's end.

A POLICEMAN'S LOT

This, then, was the town policed by the "Carmarthen Shilling" in the 1870s and 1880s. These were the streets, courts, steps and alleyways where Carmarthen's twelve policemen wal-

143

ked their beats, and for all the lively times they had in subduing the town's fighting drunks, they policed a town which was still remarkably free of crime. Whatever may be said of the improvidence and recklessness of some of the "lower orders", the townspeople's innate honesty alway prevailed over all their struggles for subsistence. Assize and Quarter Sessions calendars were invariably either empty or almost so.

Such prisoners as did come before the higher courts, though, could still be assured of stiff punishment, no matter what their ages or what their circumstances. Little Margaret Davies of Priory Street, only thirteen years old, was before the Recorder in June, 1874, charged with breaking into Thomas Arthur's grocery shop in Priory Street and stealing about eight shillings (40p), a pound of sugar and three ounces of tea, to help provide for her iron worker father, her sick mother and her five younger brothers and sisters. Strong pleas were made on her behalf for mercy after she had pleaded guilty to the crime, but the sentence of the court was that young Margaret should go to gaol *for six months, with hard labour.*

And off she went, in the company of a large policeman, through Nott Square, into Queen Street and around the corner into Spilman Street, to enter the great and terrifying gaol gates into what must have been a nightmare world to one so young.

But the rarity of crimes like this can be gauged not only by the fact that *no more than a dozen a year* were reported to the police, but also by the amount of space devoted to such a crime when it *was* reported. Eight or nine column inches were not exceptional for, say, the breaking into of a warehouse on the quay and the theft of a few shillings worth of property. And we can also gauge its rarity and novelty by the manner in which the crowds flocked to witness—and participate in—the hearing in the Guildhall of—

> "*The charge against a head milliner at Carmarthen—extraordinary scenes* : A case which aroused considerable excitment throughout Carmarthen on Wednesday of last week (June, 1896—almost within living memory) was that in which Miss Maud Perry, Head Milliner at the establishment of Messrs. W. R. Edwards and Son,

Guildhall Square, was charged with stealing a baby's cap and a piece of silk *value five shillings* (25p). When it became known that the accused lady had been taken into custody and would be tried at nine o'clock, a large number of people gathered around the Guildhall in the expectation of being able to catch a glimpse of her.

The Mayor occupied the Chair on the Magistrates' Bench. Messrs. W. R. and John Edwards were present, but did not give evidence. When they entered the court they were loudly hissed by the people at the back of the court and the Bench had to threaten to empty the court to keep order.

At the conclusion of the case the Bench retired for a few minutes and on returning the Mayor said ' We have carefully considered the evidence adduced in this case and we are unanimously of the opinion that no jury would convict upon the evidence laid before us to-day. (To the prisoner) Therefore we discharge you. '

The decision was given amid dead silence, but when it was known, a roar of cheering burst from those in court. The noise was heard by the crowd outside and instantly recognised, and for the next few minutes the scene was one of extraordinary excitement. Hats were waved and cheer after cheer resounded through the Square. Miss Perry swooned away and had to be revived with restoratives.

On emerging from the Hall she was accompanied by the crowd to Mr. Carpenter's (Stationer), the crowd meanwhile cheering and singing ' *See the conquering hero comes* '. Another detachment of the crowd went to the residence of the solicitor for the defence and raised three cheers for Mr. Walters. Mr. W. R. Edwards and his son, on the other hand, were loudly hooted as they left the court, protected by the police." (C. J.)

And for all the drunken assaults handled by the police, it was almost unknown for anyone to be killed as a result (the last time being about thirty years before), and when it did happen "Death by Misadventure" was invariably the Coroner's verdict.

The crime of murder was exceedingly rare and always involved people with a close, often family, relationship, and the outcome would fall short of a murder verdict, with a verdict of "Guilty but insane" or "Manslaughter".

There were no executions in Carmarthen for almost sixty years, between the hangings of David Evans in 1829 (a public execution) and David Rees, "The Llanelli Murderer" in March, 1888.

Executions were no longer public, but the crowds would still gather outside the gaol to share the vicarious thrill of the grim proceedings within the high, grey walls. Another job for the "Carmarthen Shilling", and they began it the day before by escorting the hangman from the railway station to the gaol through a curious and excited crowd :

> "Berry arrived in Carmarthen by the 3 o'clock train. On the journey down he was not recognised until he reached Carmarthen junction where, as he waited for a train to carry him to Carmarthen Town, a great crowd collected and gazed upon the public executioner with mingled feelings of wonderment and awe. The news quickly spread from the junction to the town station, and on arriving there he found that his fame had preceded him. As he walked to the gaol he was followed by a motley mob, who hung around the portals of the prison for some time after the executioner had disappeared from view." (C. J.)

And then there was the work of preparation—the scaffold to be tested, the condemned man to be weighed and measured so as to gauge the length and strength of the rope, a plot to be dug in the garden on the north west side of the gaol yard and a mound of quick-lime to be placed beside it to receive his prison-garbed body. All the grim ritual of the execution, reported in all of its morbid detail for the benefit of an eager public :

> " . . . the gallows were fixed up as a permanent structure. It is placed on the west side of the prison yard, next to Nott Square. The trap doors are on a level with the ground, so that the necessity of climbing up to the

drop is dispensed with. The pit is excavated to a depth of ten feet and the sides are bricked. At the side is a manhole for the use of an attendant in case of any hitch in carrying out the dread sentence of the law. From the platform to the cross bar is a distance of seven feet. Berry characterised this scaffold as one of the best he had used.

The scaffold is not a new one, having been used at Dolgelly previously for the execution of one Cadwaladr Jones for the murder of a woman in 1877. This was while Mr. Owen Thomas, the present Governor of Carmarthen Gaol was Governor there. When Dolgelly Gaol was dismantled the gallows were sent to Carmarthen. It was set up for the execution of Price, the Aberystwyth wife murderer, but Carmarthen was mercifully spared the horror of an execution by a reprieve arriving at the last moment.

The rope is what is known as a two inch rope and is made of Italian silk hemp. It has already been used for the execution of four men, one of whom was Dr. Cross, executed at Cork the other day.

The convict weighed nearly 11 stone and the drop would be about six feet and this, as a result of the experience of the executioner, would exercise a strain upon the rope of nearly 27 hundredweight. This was the same drop as was given to Nash, the Swansea murderer, who was about the same weight as Rees." (C. J.)

All was now ready, and executioner Berry drank his nightcap with the Governor in his warm and cosy living quarters, while a few yards away in the bleak and bare sick ward, at about 10 o'clock, David Rees drifted into a fitful doze to nightmare away his last hours on earth.

Tuesday morning, the 13th of March, 1888, dawned cold and grey, with streaks of watery sunshine appearing over Llangunnor Hill when David Rees awoke, dressed himself and took his breakfast of milk, bread and butter, afterwards to be joined by the Gaol Chaplain, the Rev. T. R. Walters, who remained with him until the end, preparing the crying and shaking man for his imminent meeting with his Maker—for the dread, traditional hour of 8 o'clock was but an hour and a half away.

And outside the gaol gates, Chief Constable Brown-Edwardes, mutton-chop whiskered, pill box hat at its familiar rakish angle, sword buckled on for to-day's public duty, mustered his Sergeants, David Williams and Lewis Hughes, his senior Constable, William Jones, and a half dozen others, as the crowd—thin at first—began to swell while the hour approached. Unlike their predecessors in the days of public hangings, they would have no disorder to cope with ; the quiet and sombre atmosphere inside would spill over the walls onto the watchers outside. And then the drama began :

> "At about quarter to eight the Chapel bell began to toll and the press and officials were placed in the long corridor of the prison opposite the cell. At 7.50 the executioner, Berry, appeared, unostentatiously dressed in a plain suit of dark clothes and wearing a red Turkish fez, bringing his pinnioning straps with him. The executioner is a light complexioned quiet looking man, of apparently about thirty years, with a light moustache, small short beard and whiskers and bright brown eyes, presenting altogether an appearance entirely unlike what might generally be expected of a public executioner.
>
> At three minutes to eight Berry went into the condemned cell to pinnion the arms of the convict, during which the unhappy man was crying bitterly and had to be supported by two warders. At a minute to eight the sad procession started from the cell and proceeded to the scaffold, the Chaplain reading the Burial Service.
>
> The prisoner, who appeared to walk rather weakly and was supported by Warders Howells and Thomas, appeared to be terribly distressed and seemed to be listening very attentively to the service, which was read most impressively by the Rev. T. R. Walters. He was dressed in the same clothes as he wore when placed in the dock at Carmarthen Guildhall. He was, however, not the same man ; the square shoulders had given place to a stoop, the knees were knocking together, the eyes, once

so ready to meet every glance, drooped towards the ground.

As the mournful cortege reached the top of the steps leading to the prison yard, the culprit, seeing for the first time probably the shed in which the gallows were concealed, cried "Oh Arglwydd Anwyl" ("Oh Dear Lord"). The procession on reaching the shed halted outside while the unhappy man, the executioner and warders went inside. The prisoner was placed on the centre of the trap while the rope was adjusted around his neck by Berry, and the brass ring forming the noose was placed under the left ear, the white cap then being pulled over his head.

The Chaplain all this time had continued reading the Burial Service in Welsh, in which the unhappy man joined, repeating the responses and occasionally shaking his head sadly, as if bewailing his terrible fate. At about a minute past eight o'clock, at the words "Duw a drugarha wrthyf" the lever was pulled. The drop fell and Rees was launched into eternity. As the drop fell, the black flag was hoisted on a flagstaff above the female wards facing Spilman Street.

Berry said the man never moved a limb after he fell."
(C.J.)

Rees's executioner stayed in Carmarthen for only two hours more, taking the opportunity to do a bit of shopping, followed by the inevitable crowd and escorted by several policemen. And when he had bought his mementoes of his brief visit to Carmarthen he returned to the prison, where he—

" . . . took up his coat, portmanteau and other belongings, and, passing out between two groups made up of jurymen, officials and others, he remarked *"Good morning Gentlemen. I hope you will never want me here again."* (C.J.)

It was his one and only visit.

Curiously enough, though, having gone sixty years without a single execution, Carmarthen Gaol was now to see three in the space of six years, but only one of those hanged had committed his murder in the town. In November, 1893, George

Thomas, a twenty-three years old Militia man and ex-Royal Artillery gunner from Johnstown, had murdered fifteen years old Mary Jane Jones, housekeeper to her aunt, Mrs. Rosla Dyer at "Dawelau", a small cottage between Pentremeurig Farm and the Joint Counties Lunatic Asylum.[3] It was Police Sergeant James Jones who had first word of this "most foul, cold-blooded murder", at about a quarter to ten on Sunday evening, the 19th of November. As he walked along King Street towards Nott Square :

> " . . . he was accosted by a young man named George Thomas of Johnstown who said he wished to make a statement to him. The Sergeant, little thinking of the horrible clue he was about to receive, took the man on one side and encouraged him to speak. Thomas then confessed to having killed a girl he had been keeping company with, adding that he had left her on the road near the Joint Counties Lunatic Asylum. Sergeant Jones was naturally dubious, but the unhappy man assured him that his statement was correct and that he had premeditated the deed. He was then taken to the police station.
>
> Bloodstains were noticed on his clothes and hands and no further doubt could be entertained. Not a minute was lost in visiting the spot indicated by the self-confessed murderer and in a short time Chief Constable Smith (who was now in charge of the affair) accompanied by Dr. R. L. Thomas and Sergeant James, hired a cab from the Old Plough Inn (Lammas Street) and drove up with all haste. When about a quarter of a mile from the Asylum, midway between Pentremeurig Farm and a small cottage ' Dawelau ', the anxious searchers discovered the body of a young girl lying in a large pool of fresh blood, with two gaping gashes in the throat, the head being almost severed from the body." (C.J.)

It was a crime that aroused considerable anger in the town, and it was through large and threatening crowds that Thomas was taken by large, bewhiskered policemen, first to the magistrates' court and later to the Assizes, each held in a crowded

Guildhall. He was strongly protected too, after the black-capped judge had pronounced the dread sentence " . . . to be hanged by the neck until you be dead", and he was taken by closed carriage to the nearby gaol. Any hopes he might have entertained about a last minute pardon were dashed by a telegram to the Governor from the Home Secretary, the news of which "spread like wildfire through the town, and was received in many quarters with entire approval".

Once again, the executioner was the object of a great deal of attention :

> "Shortly before three o'clock the railway station was besieged by an excited gathering of men, women and children. As soon as the train steamed into the station a rush was made over the bridge to the other platform. The carriage which Billington occupied was pointed out by a pressman who walked up to Abergwili to meet the train, and having spotted him travelled back to town in the next compartment. As the doors of the carriage were opened, the crowd formed a semi-circle around and eagerly scanned the faces of the occupants. Now and then one would shout ' There he is ' and ' That's him '. However, at last he was pointed out, walking between two farmers and for all the world he looked like a horse-dealer or, as someone remarked, ' Very horrified '. Indeed, had he not been pointed out it is a question whether the crowd would have known him.
>
> He proceeded up the platform followed by a large number of the loafers of the town. He enquired the way to the Gaol and on being informed at once set off at a brisk pace. The crowd followed quickly behind, criticising his dress and features. One woman's opinion was ' *he is a regular hangman* '. At the top of the Gaol steps there was a large assemblage of people who also joined the demonstration up to the prison gates."

And on the morning of the execution the ritual dance of death ; the dull and solemn clang of the chapel bell, the pinnioning of the condemned man's hands behind his back, the procession from the condemned cell to the gallows, the Chaplain's voice

—audible for the few seconds the procession was out in the open —"I am the resurrection and the life . . . man that is born of woman hath but a short time to live and is full of misery . . . in the midst of life we are in death . . . O Death, where is thy sting, O Grave, where is thy victory . . ." And then—

" . . . the condemned man walked straight onto the trap door, placing his feet on each side of the chalked mark which Billington had made there. He glanced up towards the cross-beam as if to see that he was directly under it. The executioner, having pinnioned the convict's feet, adjusted the noose and drew the white cap over his face. Billington then stepped off the drop, drew the bolt and the unfortunate George Thomas instantly passed into eternity, as the Chaplain uttered the words 'Lord have mercy upon us'. There was a little muscular motion after the body had dropped and then all was quiet, death appearing to have taken place instantaneously.

The body, after hanging for an hour, was raised from the pit, the rope taken off the neck, and conveyed to the treadwheel house, where it was laid out. After the inquest it was placed in a deal coffin and was interred in a garden on the north west side of the gaol, placed in a quantity of quick-lime upon which the earth was thrown." (C.J.)

The atmosphere outside the gates contrasted starkly with the bright sunshine of the crisp February morning, the crowd of four or five hundred and the watching policemen shuffling silently, necks craned towards the empty flagstaff high over the gaol gateway, waiting for what would inevitably be an anticlimax :

"As time went on, men took their watches and glanced at the bare flagstaff, calculating the number of minutes that still remained to make up the sum total of George Thomas's life. At a few minutes past eight the tolling of the 'Passing bell' was distinctly heard and almost before anyone had time to look at his watch the rope attached to the flagstaff was seen to move and the black flag appeared above the well of the entrance. There was little or no demonstration when this signal of death appeared and most of the crowd dispersed, satisfied that they had observed the only possible indication of the dreadful ceremony which had been performed in the seclusion of the prison." (C.J.)

Was it revenge they had wanted? Was it some demonstration to themselves and others that crime does not pay ? Or was it simply an "eye for an eye" ? Few, if any, of them knew. All they knew was that they had been there, close to the hand of death, close to the launching of a man into eternity.

They were there a year later when they hung Thomas Richards from Borth for murdering his friend James Davies's wife, while burgling their home, one of three small cottages known as London Place, close to Borth. It was the familiar ritual with the familiar press coverage, except perhaps for the gratuitous comment that the condemned man had put on twelve pounds in weight on the prison diet, a fact that was no doubt given its due consideration by executioner Billington as he fingered the length of Italian silk hemp and calculated the strain it was to take as Richards dropped and his neck was snapped by the carefully placed brass noose-ring.

Such are the finer points of the art of hanging.

As the crowds shuffled away from the gaol gates down Castle Hill to the Quay, or along Spilman Street towards Priory Street, or into Queen Street and to the town centre, to go about their daily routines, so the policemen would walk back to their own real world of traffic jams, obstructed pavements and people in need of all kinds of help. During the days they did what they could to ease the congestion in the streets caused by horse and cattle fairs, by horses, carriages and carts both moving and stationary, and by the age-old problems of ash heaps, carelessly tipped building materials and pavement-stacked shop wares. There was no end to their work. The policemen answered calls to family fights and locked up drunks at all hours of the day—from as early as seven o'clock in the morning when the iron and tin nightworkers broke the law to lay the foundry dust—and they did the thousand and one things that comprised their role in the keeping of a kind of order in an inherently indisciplined and uninhibited town. They were responsible for checking on the accuracy of scales and weights used in business and for collecting food samples from shops for analysis, as well as for maintaining and manning the town's fire engine.[4] They even pandered to the superstitions of the old ladies of the town that "if parties on first going out on New Year's Day happened to cast their eyes on one of the same sex as themselves, it is an unlucky and an unfavourable omen". One of their first tasks on a nineteenth century New Year's morning was to present themselves at the doors of the old ladies who had had the foresight to arrange for the old curse to be thwarted !

At night they made sure that doors were locked, that the street gas lamps were lit and extinguished at the proper times, that the streets were cleared of the late-night revellers and drunks, that the lodging houses were not too overcrowded, that no-one allowed the town's precious water supply to run to waste. And they reported when "The Town Clock don't strick all night".

Some of the flavour of those times, the sounds and the smells of those streets, and some glimpses of the daily lives of the townspeople, come out of the yellowing, brown-inked pages of such dusty old "Occurrence Books" as have survived the passing of a century. To browse through their mis-spelt entries is to walk those old streets with the "Carmarthen Shilling".

"Sunday 27th November, 1870. P.C. Rees 9[5] reports that about 11 p.m. he saw Mr. David Lloyd, Surgeon, King Street, very Drunk and besmeared with mud in Guildhall Square. He went into the passage of the (Carmarthen) Journal Office and shouted and then ran off. He also did the same in the passage of the house of Mr. T. H. Lewis, Nott Square. Quiet night—Fine Weather. David Williams, Police Sergeant."

*   *   *

"Tuesday night 20th December, 1870. There was a Supper Party at Mr. Tamplin's, The Vine, Lammas Street. The company did not break up until about 5 a.m.

154

There was no quarrelling or fighting, *but loud singing all the night*. Showers. David Williams, Police Sergeant."

*   *   *

"Saturday night 24th December, 1870. All correct during the night. *No attempt at fireworks.*[6] I have told the Day and Night Squads to Muster in their best Uniform at the Guildhall at 10.30 a.m. tomorrow (for the Mayor's procession to St. Peter's Church on Christmas Day). Frost. David Williams, Police Sergeant."

*   *   *

"Thursday night 9th February, 1871. The Ball at the (King Street) Assembly Rooms broke up at 5.30 a.m. Quiet during the night. Showers. 9 over the number in No. 1 lodging house (Quay Street) ; 2 over the number in No. 4 (Water Street). David Williams, Police Sergeant."

*   *   *

"Sunday night 19th March, 1871. P.C. Lewis No. 1[7] reports that about 11 p.m. six commercial men came through Nott Square and commenced screaming out very much, and also Queen Street and Spilman Street. He runed after them and cautioned them as to thire conduct on a 'Sunday night'. They all went to the Bush Royal Hotel. All strangers to the P.C.s. All very quiet during the Night. William Jones, No.2."[8]

*   *   *

"Saturday 27th May, 1876. P.C. No.5 John Harries[9] reports : About 8 p.m. I was on duty at the corner of Water Street and Catherine Street. I there saw Thomas Bevan, aged 22 years, a spinner, of Catherine Street. He was drunk and riotous, cursing and swearing. He

155

was calling out to everybody and challenging them to fight and at the time in a fighting attitude. I then took him into custody, when he became very violent, wilfully kicking and beating. He kicked at my legs and pulled my whiskers, also the collar of my uniform coat. Great complaints have been made about his conduct all day in the above streets."

* * *

"Saturday 22nd April, 1876. P.C. Thomas Rees reports : About 8.30 p.m. I was on duty in Lammas Street, when I was called to No. 12 Catherine Street by John, son of Howell Evans, carpenter, who told me that his father was drunk in the house and that he was breaking the furniture up to pieces. I went there and found Evans was on the floor, being held down by force by one David Thomas, shoemaker, who lives next door. I asked Thomas to let him get up and he did so, and as soon as he was on his feet he swore at me and struck me a violent blow on the nose which caused my nose to bleed very much. I then took hold of him, and his wife Sarah begged me not to take him to the station house. He was drunk and very noisy."

* * *

"Tuesday 6th June, 1876. P.C. Berian Rees No. 4[10] reports : About 6 p.m. I was on duty in King Street. I saw David Lewis, butcher, Brynteg, alias ' Dai Shilling ', drunk when in charge of a horse and trap. He was driving down King Street at a furious pace. When opposite Dr. Lloyd's he wheeled the horse round to the left and drove it on the pavement, to the danger of passengers. He had no hat on his head at the time."

* * *

"Friday 3rd November, 1876. Chief Constable's report for Magistrates concerning the letting off of fireworks in the public streets of the town : I have to report that on Wednesday last the 1st of November, 1876, a large crowd of men, women and children persisted ni letting off fireworks in different parts of the town, but more particularly in Guildhall Square. When I found that remonstrance had no effect on the people, I issued a general order to the police instructing them to take down the names of all parties in the act of letting fireworks off, a list of which I give you below. I earnestly hope that you will order summonses to be taken out against all of the parties, as it seems to be an impression among the public that such conduct is allowed at election times and will not be punished by the Magistrates."

The list of twenty-seven names appended to this entry gives some idea of the cross-section of the townspeople who came together to share in the noise and excitement of an election or any other event at which they could give vent to their traditional Carmarthen boisterousness. There were shop-assistants, tin-workers, a schoolmaster, printers from the *Carmarthen Journal* and *Welshman* newspapers, a commercial traveller, labourers, publicans, a railway engine driver, a tailor, a groom and others of unknown occupation.

*   *   *

"Tuesday 17th April, 1877. Sergeant David Williams reports : At 9.40 a.m. I saw David Beynon, nailer aged 37 years, of Dan y Banc, coming from towards Jackson's Lane to the corner of King and Queen Streets. He was very drunk and as he passed me he said in Welsh ' Good morning Sergeant Williams '. I told him to go to his lodgings. He said he would not go. I then took him into custody and when opposite the Town Clerk's Office he resisted and fell on the ground, cursing and swearing. The ex-Mayor then came and persuaded him to come quiet. He came all the way to the station house by the the side of the ex-Mayor."

*   *   *

"Saturday 30th June, 1877. The Chief Constable reports : At 10.25 a.m. I saw David Lewis, butcher, on horseback, very drunk in Saint Catherine Street and refusing to leave the front door of the ' Tanners ' public house[11] when requested to do so by P.C. J. Harries No.5. He called for a glass of beer which was given him by the barmaid. When I prevented him drinking it he rode his horse onto the pavement and a large crowd collected around the front door of the public house."

*   *   *

"Saturday night 28th July, 1877. P.C. William Jones reports—At 11 p.m. I was at the Tinworks entrance gate and there heard a row and screaming lower down Priory Street. I ran there at once and saw James Evans, tin-finer, No. 45 Priory Street, drunk and had been fighting with parties in a large crowd of people around him. His brother came there and took him home, with women. Through his conduct he excited the street and caused a crowd to collect. In the crowd I saw Joseph Bowen, furnace-man at the tinworks, of No. 95 Priory Street, very drunk with his coat off and wanting to fight with anyone. Then he was taken home with his neighbours. *Being ' paynight ', tinworks, and supper at the ' Boat and Anchor ' public house.*"

*   *   *

"Saturday 28th July, 1877. P.C. Evan Evans No.3[12] reports—About 10.20 p.m. I was coming out from the Theatre and outside the door I saw James Lewis, alias Jim Pig, Priory Street, pig dealer. He came up to me and said ' Damn the bloody bobbies. Your oul' Superintendent is gone (Chief Constable Frank D. Lewis had resigned after only ten months), and you will have to go soon after him ' and with that he kicked me on the leg. I then took him into custody and a large crowd collected, and in the scuffle his brother and some others rescued him from me. I then went to the police station and reported this to Sergeant Williams. When I was

158

coming out I again met Lewis and his brother William, and he rushed on to me saying to his brother ' Here he is again ' and he took hold of me by the collar. I then took him into custody with the assistance of P.C. Thomas No. 6.''[13]

* * *

"Wednesday 15th August, 1877. P.C. John Harries No. 5 reports—I went to serve a summons on David Davies, Hawker, Cambrian Place. When I saw him he was drunk. I told him I had a summons for him. He said ' If you will come inside this yard I will set the bitch on you '. He then loosed the bitch and set her on me. He then threw a brick and nearly struck me with it. He then ran into the house.''

* * *

"Tuesday 14th August, 1877. Row in Jackson's Lane. P.C. William Jones reports—About 9.5 p.m. as the night P.Cs was proceeding up Jackson's Lane we saw a crowd of people outside of David Harries, shoemaker's, door, and Mrs. Harries in the Lane screaming out ' Oh, the drunken whore. I caught her in the house on the floor with my husband.' She ordered me to turn her out. We rose the woman up from the floor and turned her out of the Lane. She is Mrs. Rees's daughter, the baker, of Jackson's Lane. She was very drunk. The husband was gone. We did not see him.''

* * *

"Friday 14th Sptember, 1877. Sergeant Lewis Hughes reports: At 12 noon yesterday I received information that Patrick Donaghue, Mill Street, hawker, came to town on the last train about 10.30 p.m. on Wednesday and that he fell down in Little Bridge Street and fell asleep. He woke there at 2.30 a.m. and all his clothes had been taken off him except shirt, waistcoat and stockings. Basket and contents missing. We found his boots about ten yards from where he was lying, and found his trow-

159

sers (sic) in the house of Benjamin Lewis, Bridge Street, coracleman, the purse in the pockets and no money in it. Several of the missing articles has been found and restored to the informant, he being too drunk on the night in question to know when or where he lost them."

*   *   *

"Thursday 6th December, 1877. David Williams, Sergeant, reports : Between 2 and 4 p.m. I warned and cautioned the following parties for not to carry an *effigy* called ' Mary Wen Lawen ' about the streets, as complaints had been made to the Mayor and other Magistrates to stop it—namely John and George Evans, Steam Mill (by Dan y Banc) alias Gilberts, Thomas Jones alias ' Tom y Llyfor ', David Davies alias ' Dai Shyr Gaer ', William Davies, Saint Catherine Street."

*   *   *

"Thursday 11th April, 1878. P.C. William Jones reports—Drunkenness in Nott Square. About 7 p.m. I saw Mr. W. R. Morgan, boot and shoe warehouse, Lower Market Street, very drunk and standing by Mrs. Daws, confectioner, King Street. He crossed the other side of the street, went along the pavement in Nott Square, and at the corner of Jenkins, shoemaker, he met Old Jem the Oysterman, and there would have oysters of him, and catching hould of his basket of oysters. By this time a crowd was collecting. Got Old Jem away and saw Mr. Morgan into the house."

*   *   *

"Friday 10th May, 1878. P.C. John Arthur No. 7[14] reports—Drunk and Riotous and assaulting the Police. At 8.30 p.m. I was on duty in Catherine Street when I saw Mary Vaughan, wife of Albert Vaughan, painter, St. Catherine Street, drunk and using abusive language and a crowd collecting around her. She now went inside the door and stood on the door and commenced to curse and swear towards me and her husband. He was drunk. I caught hold of her for to take her into custody, but I could not as her husband was rescuing her. I then left her and on my way out of the passage she caught hold of a teapot of hot tea and threw the teapot and tea over me. I then with the assistance of John E. Morgan, washerman, 57 Priory Street, and several Militia men, took her out of the house. Her husband was then trying to rescue her, but he was held down by Militia men. In the meantime my Sergeant (David) Williams came, and with the assistance of Mr. Morgans and several Militia men we took her to the station house and locked her up. Had to carry her all the way."

* * *

"Wednesday 6th February, 1878. Drunk and Incapable in Blue Street. P.C. William Jones reports—About 11.30 a.m. I was called down to Blue Street by Mr. D. B. Edwards, merchant of Wellfield Road, who complained that One-eyed Mucumaskey, alias ' Shoemaker ', Quay Street, was drunk and incapable, cursing and swearing in Blue Street. I rose him up and took him to the station house and locked him up."

* * *

"Saturday 27th April, 1878. The Chief Constable reports P. C. Jonathan Arthur No. 7 for being drunk whilst on duty in Lammas Street at 5.45 p.m. P.C. Jones No. 8[15] had called my attention to Arthur whom he accused of having cursed and swore and using other insulting language to him. Seeing that Arthur was unfit to remain on duty I ordered him home. He refused to go, saying ' You may take the bloody coat if you like '. He also turned to P.C. Jones, saying ' I'll knock your bloody head off in about two minutes. You are more drunk than I am.' I then ordered him home, telling him that if he did not go he would be locked up for the night."[16]

* * *

"Saturday 25th May, 1878. Sergeant Lewis Hughes reports that he visited Lammas Street beat about 7.45 p.m. and saw P.C. Rees D. Jones No. 4[17] coming out of P.C. Rees No. 9's house. Came towards him, he saw that he was under the influence of liquor. He (Jones) then ran after some boys and took a hoop from one of them in Gas Lane (now Morfa Lane). Sergeant Hughes then told him to take the hoop to the police station house. He did not, but walked up and down the street with the hoop in his hand and a crowd collected in the street and shouting after him. He was at once sent to the police station house, then to his lodging house and off duty."

*   *   *

"Tuesday 25th June, 1878. P.C. Stacey No. 1[18] reports that he received information at 6.45 p.m. from Mary Edwards, 15 Waterloo Terrace, that whilst making hay in a field belonging to Mr. Griffiths the currier, she left a bottle half full of ginger beer in the hedge. David Owens, the son of John Owens of Friar's Park, found the bottle, drank the contents and made urine in the bottle, part of which she drank.'

*   *   *

"Monday 8th July, 1878. P.C. W. Stacey reports that he was on duty in Priory Street from 9.30 p.m. till 12.15 a.m. There were large crowds of people about the street and about 11 p.m. someone threw an effigy from Miss Jones's field into the street, of which I took possession and brought to the police station, and with great difficulty, assisted by P.C. Harries No. 5 we dispersed them and seen all quiet."

*   *   *

"Wednesday 7th July, 1880. Narrow Escape at a Funeral. Sergeant Williams reports that at 12.30 p.m. this day he saw a funeral coming down Lower Market Street, a hearse with one horse, containing the remains

of a child of John Davies, Tailor, Spilman Street, driven
by John Davies, ostler at the ' Plough Inn ' Lammas
Street, followed by a mourning fly with one horse
driven by John Richards, post boy, Spilman Street, containing John Davies, his wife and two of their children.
When nearly opposite the Town Clerk's Office the horse
that Richards drove took fright and bolted off furiously
and came in contact with the hearse, throwing Richards
from his seat onto the pavement, still holding fast to the
reins till he was stopped in Guildhall Square.   Mrs.
Davies then came out of the fly and nearly fainted and
refused to go any further in the fly and walked along
with her husband after the hearse to St. David's Church
Yard."

*   *   *

"Sunday 3rd October, 1880.   P.C. David Nicholas
No. 2[19] reports that he visited the manure heaps at
1.15 p.m. and found all correct."

*   *   *

"Tuesday 26th October, 1880.   Burning ' Effigies ' in
Priory Street : P.C. Thomas Rees No. 9 reports that at
8.30 p.m. he was informed by Thomas Arthur, grocer,
Priory Street, that some parties had burned the effigies
of David Jones, widower, and Anne, wife of Thomas
Lewis, both of Priory Street. He went there at once and
ascertained that some lads had carried the effigies which
was on fire from Old Priory Road as far as the ' Emlyn
Castle ' public house and someone in the crowd saw the
police coming and the crowd dispersed."[20]

*   *   *

"P.C. Thomas Jones No. 3[21] reports that while visiting
Greenhill at 12.40 a.m. the night watchman at the
brewery reported to him that about 10.45 p.m. a gang
of seven men came to the brewery and knocked demanding the door to be opened to get beer. The night man
refused to open the door and they began kicking and

163

swearing they would break the windows if the door was not opened. Mr. Talbot Norton,[22] together with Miss Norton, then came to his assistance and they found one of the men hiding under a cart. They had him out and he gave his name as Richard Williams, alias ' Dick Yard Fawr ', Cambrian Place. He was very impudent to Mr. Norton and told him they would be in the brewery before the morning in spite of him and his watchman."

* * *

"Friday night 30th September, 1881. P.C. William Stacey No. 1 reports that he in company with P.C. Harries No. 5 went to St. Catherine Street and there saw David Jones, alias ' Dai Shoemaker ' of the above street, drunk, cursing and swearing towards some parties in Davies's yard. We went to him and asked him to go into the house and be quiet. He did go in but came out again at once and commenced again making use of the most abusive language towards the police saying that *he would kill every bugger of them as he would only get fourteen days for it.* We then requested him to go to the house again. He refused, we took him into custody and we with the assistance of P.C. Nicholas had to handcuff him and strap his legs and carry him all the way to the station."

* * *

"Thursday 31st August, 1882. P.C. W. Stacey No. 1 reports that at 7.50 a.m. he saw David Phillips, cattle dealer, with two other men driving some cattle through Guildhall Square towards Lammas Street, and when opposite Phillips Druggist, 2 Dark Gate, two of the cattle went into the shop and by getting them out they broke a dispensing glass case, counter glass case and frame, shop glass case and frame, a counter and several other things. The cattle belonged to Phillips, nephew of Samuel Phillips, ' Three Salmons ', Water Street."

* * *

"Sunday 10th December, 1882. P.C. Thomas Davies No. 4 reports that he done duty this day in Johnstown from *6.45 a.m. to 9 a.m.* and from 2 p.m. to 5 p.m. The police was ordered there by Mr. Superintendent (Chief Constable) James to watch the public houses, which he did very carefully, but he did not see nothing, but the occupants of both houses were watching the movements of the police *and seeming quite uneasy.*"[23]

*   *   *

"Saturday night 1st October, 1881. P.C. James Jones No. 8 reports that about 11.45 p.m. he, assisted by the Chief Constable, took into custody Michael Madigan of Mill Street, labourer, charged with being drunk and riotous in Mill Street. Madigan asked the Chief Constable to be allowed a few minutes to beat P.C. Harries No. 5 (also present) and that he would willingly take three months for it."

*   *   *

"Friday 13th January, 1882. P.C. David Nicholas No. 2 reports that about 5.40 p.m. he was called down to the Quay and he was informed that Eleanor Holmes was goying to commit suicide by drownding herself. He went there and saw her in a boat with two men houlding her. They tey her with a rope and took her up. He then with her huspand took her into the ' Ship and Castle ' lodging house, Quay Street, and told her huspand to take care of her, and then she came quiate."

*   *   *

"Sunday 29th January, 1882. P.C. Thomas Davies No. 4 reports that he was on duty in St. Peter's Church about 6.30 p.m. and there saw J. M. Allison, Veterinary Surgeon, Spilman Street. He was drunk and walked into the Church from King Street. He was stopped at the door by W. B. Jones, Parish Clerk. Then he put on his hat and rising up his walking stick commenced talking very loud and annoying people that was passing into Church."

*   *   *

"Sunday 22nd April, 1883. *Cemetery Visited.* P.C. Thomas Rees No. 9 reports that he patrolled the Cemetery from 2.40 p.m. to 3.45 p.m. *Found all quiet.*"

"FIRE ! FIRE !"

For virtually the whole of its history, the Borough Police Force was the Fire Brigade as well. Assisted by a few "Auxilliaries", the whole force would turn out when the town fire bell rang, day or night. Not only they, but the whole town came running to see the fun as the steaming engine was man-hauled out of Cambrian Place or a frantic search was made for horses (either those of the town ash carts or some borrowed from the town's coaching inns) if the fire was further afield. The wonder was that the fire engine got to any fire while it was still burning. The search for horses was a sure guarantee that the fire would be out before it arrived !

When the Borough Police Force was formed in 1836, an economy occurred to the town governors ; they could save the seven shillings (35p) a week fireman's retainer and give the job to the police for nothing. They paid rather less attention to the state of the engine, though, and it took a glorious fiasco enacted before a huge and appreciative audience to persuade them that money would have to be spent.

On a beautiful June day in 1846, the word spread like wildfire (perhaps an unfortunate simile in this tinder-box town) that the police were going to test the engine in Guildhall Square and the people flocked to join in the fun. Chief Constable Edwin Young, his Sergeant John Hill George, and his Constables Nicholas Martin, Robert Awberry, Frederick Rees, Joseph Thomas, Miles Davies and David Rees, solemnly marched up from Cambrian Place pulling the fire-pump into Guildhall Square, where the Mayor and Corporation waited

166

to be impressed. They connected the leather hose to the fire-plugs and to the cheers of the assembled multitude began to pump, the Sergeant pointing the nozzle to a high building and the Chief Constable calling out the commands.

Nothing. Not even a trickle. Followed by the hoots and jeers of the crowd, the Mayor, Corporation, Police Force and fire pump went up to Spilman Street to try their luck there. This time, as all concerned held their breath, there was a splutter and a splash and—cheers—a spout of water. And what a spout. Right up to the top of the ground floor window of Morris's Bank building. Lord help anyone on the first floor if there was a real fire, for try as they might—cheered on by the crowd—they could get it no higher. The *Carmarthen Journal* described the exercise as "a most miserable failure" and declared that "it must now be apparent to every person that the engine is not only inefficient but worthless !"

Backed by funds provided by worried insurance companies and aided by a letter of advice from Mr. Braidwood, Captain of the London Fire Brigade, they bought the new equipment and now they were ready for anything.

Or were they ? Things were not so bad when the fire was close at hand, because the first men to respond would run to the scene with a hose-reel and hand pump to put at least a small jet on the flames, while the main body followed with the engine. But when the call was received to a fire any distance out of town and horses were needed for the fire engine, the drama some-times took on a kind of black humour :

"Saturday 21st October, 1882. Sergeant David Williams reports that at 10.10 last night information was received at the police station that the fire engine was required at Derllys Farm, that the haggard was on fire. He in company with Mr. (Chief Constable) James went at once to the Engine House and there met several of the police force and others, and having put the shaft etc. in order, took it so far as the ' Boar's Head ' Hotel, where we had to wait for nearly half an hour before we could get horses, after which there was one brought out from the ' Boar's Head ' Hotel and two from Mr. Bland's

167

stable. When we started, it was about 10.45 p.m. Some of the harness having broken caused some delay.

When about fifty yards from Penffordlas (two miles from the Boars Head), the shaft horse got out of harness causing the fall of the Chief Constable, who had driven all the way. He was assisted to Penffordlas and shortly afterwards was attended by W. L. Hughes, Surgeon, who found that he had dislocated his collar bone and had it put in its place, and he was taken home in a trap some time in the morning.

We then proceeded on to Derllys, arriving there about 11.30 p.m. Finding the hayrick on fire, the engine was placed near the pond or brook and two lengths of suction pipe attached to the fire engine, and fastened at the end was a copper strainer placed in a basket in the brook, and then four lengths of leather pipes was attached to reach the hay. A number of persons then pumped and a good supply of water was kept pouring on the rick until about 3 a.m. when the fire was quite extinguished."

The last of Carmarthen's "Fire steamers" was brought to the town in 1896, and the arrival of this gleaming, brass-bedecked jewel of the steam-powered fire-pump age was an occasion for a huge turn-out. Placed symbolically before the Guildhall steps, it formed the centre-piece for a unique photograph in which the whole Borough Police Force, the Fire Auxilliaries and the admiring townspeople were brought together for the benefit of posterity. The cheeky little boys of the town peer at us from between the wheels of the engine with eyes that boast laughingly of the trick they are playing on the stern-faced arm of the law flanking the machine.

The newspaper report on the event captures just about every facet of the Carmarthen temperament—the townspeople's high spirits, their sense of humour, their gregariousness and their delight in any opportunity to make the heart of their town a scene of celebration of anything from a famous victory to . . . well . . .

"The trial of the New Fire Engine at Carmarthen : About as dense a crowd of people as Carmarthen could

168

Ivy Bush Royal Hotel,
CARMARTHEN.

The Ivy Bush Hotel in Spilman Street, towards the end of the century

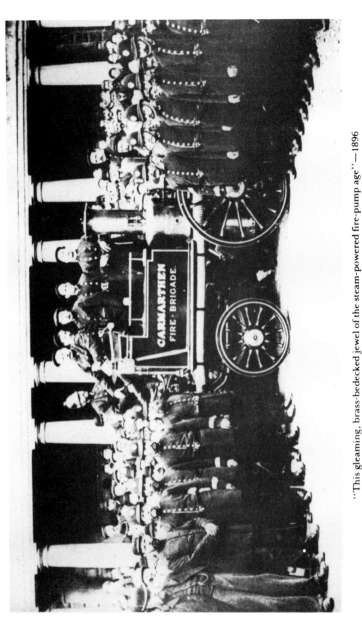

"This gleaming, brass-bedecked jewel of the steam-powered fire-pump age" —1896

Left to right: Jonathan Morgan (Surveyor); Chief Constable Thomas Smith; Constables No. 9 Thomas Rees,
No. 4 Thomas Davies, No. 2 Thomas Phillips; Sergeant James Jones; Firemen D. Rogers, William Finch,
George Rogers, C. H. Carpenter, William Thomas, D. Evans, H. Baskerville; Sergeant John Harries;
Constables No. 8 John Thomas, No. 7 William Davies, No. 1 Thomas Jacob Thomas, No. 5 David Lodwick,
No. 6 Edward Edmund Burnhill

produce assembled in Guildhall Square on Wednesday afternoon (the 8th of April, 1896) to witness the trial of the new fire engine. For about three quarters of an hour the excitement in the Square was about as keen as that attending a genuine fire. Sharp at 3 o'clock the fire engine, a dainty looking construction, was wheeled into position in front of the Guildhall and—surrounded by members of the fire brigade (who looked very heroic in their uniform) and surmounted by members of the police in charge of Superintendent Smith—was photographed by Mr. Henry Howell amidst an appropriate and respectful silence.

The camera done with, the police and firemen laid hands on the engine and moved it back and fore and shifted it into position until its saucy little brass funnel looked quite aggrieved. The liveliest interest was taken by the crowd in the subsequent proceedings in which a number of the members of the Town Council joined. A continuous flow of pungent criticism was contributed by the spectators, and offers of advice as to the best method of handling a hose and screwing a nut were not wanting. 'Wel, ar f'enaid i,' screamed the proud possessor of a pair of red whiskers, 'Look at old . . . He don't know the way to handle a spanner no more than a monkey!' 'Ay' remarked a tall man, who leant on the shoulder of a little man, 'It's a good job there is no fire. Half Carmarthen would be burnt down before they could get the steam up.' 'Wel, di'awch ariod—turn the hose round man' he shouted, his excitement getting the better of him. 'Go it boys' yelped another little man who was evidently a member of the unemployed, 'Another threepence for the ratepayers!' 'Look at old . . . Ooh, if he'd only give me the nozzle,' bawled a short navvy. 'Chipped Potatoes All Hot' was another remark, which sent the crowd into convulsions.

Meanwhile the town hall clock was so excited at the proceedings that it forgot to strike (strick ?) the half hour (a fact which escaped general notice) and the brass weathercock heaped contempt upon the crowd below.

169

By this time, however, the members of the fire brigade and police under the skilful supervision of one of Messrs. Shand and Mason's (the fire engine manufacturers) employees, had been doing good work and had got the fire engine into action. At 29 minutes past three, the Mayor placed a match to the furnace of the engine and immediately a cloud of dense brown smoke roared out of the engine funnel and filled the square.

In exactly six minutes steam was ' up ' and the engine as though stung into unusual activity by the remarks of the crowd, panted and snorted at a furious rate, and a stream of water from the hose pipe crept up the Guildhall and suddenly shot up into the air to an immense height—to the complete demoralisation of the jackdaws who had been watching the proceedings with intelligence and fled in all directions.

The front of the Guildhall was thoroughly washed, and so were a few people who stood near the hall steps and had seemed to regard the experiments with their kind approval. The engine was afterwards taken to the Quay, where further experiments were made and there appears to be no doubt that the new fire engine is a complete success." (C.J.)

For over twenty years that engine served the town well. But it was to meet an ignominious end. The demise of the horse-hauled "steamer" came in a quite dramatic and even hilarious manner, as the Carmarthen Fire Brigade was dragged, almost reluctantly it seems, into the twentieth century age of the internal combustion engine.

At eight o'clock on a bright Sunday morning in August, 1918, the telephone rang in the station house. It was a call for help from the County Police ; there was a fire at the Cawdor Arms, Newcastle Emlyn—seventeen miles away, or four hours by horse-drawn fire engine.

Sergeant David Jones, himself a Newcastle Emlyn man, received the call and went to tell the Chief Constable.

Now this was a question for the Mayor, whose permission was needed before the borough policemen and their fire engine could venture across the borough boundary. It was half an hour before "His Worship the Mayor was consulted as to the expediency or otherwise of the expedition and he consented"[24] and the Chief Constable was able to sound the town fire bell. He was pleased to be able to report later to the Watch Committee that "The members of the Brigade were at their posts *within half an hour* of the call." They were, of course, accompanied by a huge crowd of people, who packed John Street and Cambrian Place, straining their necks to see the gleaming appliance brought out of its building.

The engine was got ready, but since it was obvious that horse power alone would not get them there before the hotel was razed to the ground, a lorry was hired from Mr. Page, a local haulage contractor. The lorry was brought to the fire engine house and hitched up, and at ten o'clock (two hours after the telephone call !) the lorry, fire engine, policemen, auxilliaries— and half the town—headed off for Priory Street and Abergwili on the long trek to the burning Cawdor Arms.

Whether Mr. Page's lorry was an old one or whether it was poorly maintained is not clear. What is clear is that it had got no further than the Bronwydd turn at Abergwili (at the borough boundary) when "the engine became so overheated as to become dangerous". The cavalcade halted, as the radiator of the lorry vied with the snorting fire-steamer in producing the clouds of steam which hid the embarrassing sight from the inquisitive gaze of the cattle lazing in the summer sunshine in the roadside fields.

But Mr. Page obviously knew his lorries well, because he had taken the precaution of bringing up a second one in the rear. A rapid switch got the cavalcade moving slowly up the hill, through Cwmgwili and Conwyl Elfed—but the steeply winding road leading them to Cwmduad proved just too much, and amidst another vast cloud of steam they ground to a halt once again.

So it was back to horse power and, the war still being on, salvation was at hand in the shape of an Army Remount Depot It was while the horses were being harnessed to the shafts of the fire steamer—three and a half hours after the frantic message that "the hotel and adjacent premises were in danger of being enveloped and destroyed"—that a horse-messenger reached the sweating but still determined fire brigade and helpers. It was hardly to be wondered at that he carried the word that the fire was under control and they were no longer needed !

And so the disconsolate party limped back to Carmarthen, leaving a steaming lorry at Cwmduad and passing its derelict brother as they crossed the borough boundary under the high afternoon sun. Past straggling groups of silent watchers, they clattered into Cambrian Place and took their embarrassment—along with the now cooling steamer—into the safe haven of the engine house.

The day of the fire-horse was over. The Watch Committee acceded to the Chief Constable's view that "under the present regime the utility of the present appliances is negligible" and that "Where there is a raging fire in a dwellinghouse and every means of escape cut off, with a motor engine the escapes could be taken with the fire engine without any inconvenience." They agreed to buy one.

And to add insult to injury, they sent a bill to the "Newcastle Emlyn Authorities" for 3 pounds 13 shilling (£3.65)—1 pound 13 shillings for the men . . . and £2 for the hire of the motor lorries !

Their reply is not recorded.

NOTES

1Lewis Hughes, a native of Aberystwyth, joined in March, 1865, at the age of 35 after 3 years in the Cardiganshire Force, preceded by nearly 16 years in one of the Staffordshire Regiments. He retired on a Sergeant's pension of 18 shillings (90p) a week on 21st March, 1891, and was then living at 1 St. Catherine Street.

2Compare this with the last thirty-four years of its existence (1913 to 1947) when the figure was only twenty-six.

3Now Saint David's Mental Hospital.

4See "Fire ! Fire !" later in this Chapter.

5Thomas Rees, ex-Cardiganshire policeman, served in Carmarthen from January 1868 to May 1897, retiring on pension as a Constable. He lived in Sawmill Terrace, on the quay.

6This was Christmas Eve, the traditional "Torch Night", and this was the year when the tradition died—by order of the Mayor.

7David Lewis served from July 1866 until 1875.

8The first man to serve long enough to draw a pension, he joined in 1849 and served for thirty years. See his escapade in Chapter 6, page 90.

9John Harries, a farm servant of Llangynnog, Carmarthen, joined the force in November 1869, was promoted Sergeant in June 1888 (replacing David Williams on his retirement) and retired on pension in April 1903. He died at his home in Wellfield Road in 1918 at the age of 78. Before joining he worked on the estate which now comprises the Coomb Cheshire Home near Carmarthen.

10Served from June 1875 until 1878, when he resigned.

11Still open for business by the Market gates.

12Served from June 1875 until June 1878, when he 'absconded', leaving both his wife and family and the police force high and dry!

13William Thomas joined in May 1877 and was still serving when he died in March 1885.

14Served from March 1877 to February 1888 when he resigned after facing one of his many disciplinary hearings for drunkenness.

15James Jones, a shoemaker from Newcastle Emlyn, joined in April 1874. He was promoted Sergeant in March 1891, but required to resign in 1902 for "Being absent from a fire", the last of a number of disciplinary offences.

16Jonathan Arthur served on for another eleven years after this incident.

17Rees David Jones had only served for four months, and this escapade ended his short career.

18William Stacey joined in June 1875 but had to resign through ill-health in 1895. He died in 1919.

19David Nicholas served from May 1879 until November 1883, when he was discharged for drunkenness.

20This was the traditional use of the Ceffyl Pren—to expose adulterers.

21A farm servant from Narberth, Pembrokeshire, he joined in 1878 but was obliged to retire through ill-health in 1897. He died at his home, 13 Waterloo Terrace, in 1937—at the age of 84.

22The owner of the brewery.

23Sunday, and a *dry* day in Carmarthen.

24Chief Constable's reports to the Watch Committee; "Museum" Collection, Dyfed County Record Office.

CHAPTER TEN

AN ARMY VAST, THE TEMPERANCE HOST

IN the 1880s an influential national weekly pronounced Carmarthen to be "possessed of the most drunken inhabitants in Wales". It was a claim disputed by many ministers of religion and other local worthies on the basis of the relatively small number of cases of drunkenness and drunken assaults (a hundred or so a year) and of illegally selling liquor (little more than a dozen a year) coming before the magistrates. But we have seen enough to know that they were deluding themselves, turning a blind eye to the reality outside their churches and chapels, their offices and their shops. Although drunken violence was almost exclusive to the coraclemen, the labouring classes, the prostitutes and the "lower orders" generally, drink itself was deeply rooted in the traditions of the town at all levels. Fair days and mart days filled the hundred or so inns and alehouses to capacity from morning to night with farmers, drovers, landowners and others connected with the agricultural trade of the county. Drunks staggered through streets lined with carts, traps and wagons, while their mounted counterparts terrified the crowds by galloping or driving at breakneck speed through Guildhall Square and the other thoroughfares of the town. The drunken driver is no modern phenomenon, except in the more deadly nature of his conveyance !

Any occasion—the races, the river regatta, the Hunt Ball, the Tradesmen's Ball, the Mayor's Ball, and that traditional opportunity for drunken revelry, Christmas Eve—would do. Not even funerals were exempt. If many a present-day Welsh funeral is the next thing to an Irish "Wake" it is merely a relic, a pale reflection, of the eighties, when the situation was such that the "Funeral Reform Association" felt obliged to take upon itself "the encouragement of moderation in all burial, funeral and mourning observances. It strives by sermons, addresses, public meetings, the distribution of pamphlets and leaflets, and by all the means in its power to influence public opinion in the direction of simple and seemly Christian burial."

And now another old Carmarthen tradition reasserted itself. Even though they had passed off comparatively quietly in recent years, local and parliamentary elections were once again accompanied by much drunken violence. In court hearings following the municipal elections of 1875, for instance, one of the magistrates, Alderman John Thomas, found it hard to understand why only one person appeared before them for drunkenness, when—

> ". . . if the police had done their duty there would have been some forty persons at least brought up on charges of drunkenness and fighting.
>
> Mr. John Lewis Williams : ' The town was in a disgraceful state yesterday. I never remember seeing so many drunken persons about the streets. '
>
> The Town Clerk : ' The day's proceedings were a disgrace in the town. The incessant discharge of fireworks and the affrays in the street were terrifying to all respectable people. It was a disgraceful scene all day and those responsible for giving the men the drink and who ought to know better ought to be ashamed of themselves. ' "[1] (C.J.)

The ministers of the town put much of the trouble down to the fact that the contenders in the elections gave away so much drink to those who might be persuaded to vote for them. Shades of William Paxton !

When Lord Emlyn addressed a public meeting in the Guildhall in the run-up to the 1885 General Election, there was almost a repeat of the indoor violence of 1831, with a large proportion of the audience shouting and fighting, and the police powerless to quell the disturbance. One cry from the crowd spoke volumes : "How do the fishery laws stand for the people, come to that sir ?" Yes, the coraclemen were in there somewhere !

After the meeting, Hall Street and Guildhall Square were packed with a hostile mob, through which Lord Emlyn was taken by policemen who received a goodly number of bruises in thus running the gauntlet. When polling took place on Monday the 30th of November, the three booths in the Guildhall were besieged by the mob and there were many fights :

> "The rowdyism commenced on Friday night and was continued throughout Saturday. It is not surprising that the authorities decided to call in extra police.
> On Monday morning, about eighteen stalwart men belonging to the Swansea Police Force put in an appearance. They were not of a great deal of service. In fact the crowd somewhat took advantage of their want of knowledge of the ways, manners and passions of the local roughs and handled them somewhat inhospitably, so that *the borough police had to interfere to protect their brethren* !" (C.J.)

As for the comparatively few who found their way into the courts, they were usually the ones who could not get home under their own steam or who chose to assault the police. Arrest was a last resort, as indeed it still is. As we have seen, the police occurrence and the night report books reflect this, the latter with such terse yet all-embracing comments as "There were several rows and fights during the night and the police prevented many fights and disturbances in Blue Street and Dame Street", and "Several rows about the streets this night" . . . but with no prisoners to show for it. And as if Carmarthen did not have enough home-grown trouble, the eight thousand or so tramps who passed through the town every year added to the press of people supporting the thriving trade in beer and spirits which gave Carmarthen its dubious status as the drinking capital of Wales.

There was no shortage, either, of suggestions from the ministers of religion in the town that the police were too fond themselves of the bottle and too closely involved with "The Trade" to be expected to display any more enthusiasm than they did for tackling the drink problem !

Perhaps the view of a man new to the town can give us a more objective view. A Salvation Army Officer who moved to Carmarthen from Swansea in 1892 was appalled, particularly at the total disregard of the law prohibiting the Sunday opening of pubs in Wales. As he told his audience at the weekly meeting of the "Carmarthen Total Abstinence Society"—

". . . he was sorry to see Carmarthen's state on the Lord's Day. During the last two Sundays he saw more drunkenness in our town than he had seen in Swansea for six months. It made no difference where he visited drunken persons were to be seen." (C.J.)

His words moved another temperance worker to write :

"As one who has taken an active part in the temperance crusade for the last ten years, I will fearlessly say that Carmarthen has never been in such a drunken state as during the past six weeks. Drink can be had in every part of the town and the mock carrying out of our licensing laws is but a mere farce.

Churches of Carmarthen ; arise fron. your slumber and put down this damning, murderous and accursed drink traffic which is anihilating our dear old native town." (C.J.)

Murderous ? If the advocates of temperance were accused of exaggerating the evils of drink they could always point to the example of the murder by Henry Jones of his little daughter. Jones, a 36 year old milk vendor, lived at 8 Blue Street with his wife and two small daughters, and one day in December, 1887, he had a row with his wife about her ill-treatment of six year old Annie Jane in the cow shed behind their home. And then :

"Between four and five in the afternoon, Police Sergeant Lewis Hughes, hearing that a man had murdered his child, went down to the house and there found Jones sitting in the kitchen on a settle with his child on his lap with her throat cut from ear to ear. The man was fondling and carressing the child saying ' My child, my child, I did it. Come here my child.'

A good deal of excitement was manifested in the town throughout the day in connection with the sad affair. Crowds assembled in Guildhall Square and the streets adjoining to watch the prisoner being taken from the police station to the Guildhall for the opening of the magisterial enquiry. There was no hostile demonstration against the prisoner. The feeling was not so much bitterness against the accused as horror at the crime and pity for the perpetrator. Indeed ' Drink Again ' is the verdict which many of the townspeople pass as to the causes of the crime, drink intensifying other things which might be expected to lead to rash deeds." (C. J.)

There were similar scenes when Jones was brought up for trial at the next Carmarthen Assizes, when the expected verdict of "Guilty but insane" was returned and he was taken back to the County Gaol to be transferred to Broadmoor. This case was cited for a long time by the temperance people as an awful example of the evils of drink.

So desperate were the borough council to be seen to be tackling the problem seriously that they even thought of recruiting a body of plain clothes men, independent of the police force, to snoop on the town's pubs and root out the Sunday drinkers, provoking an anti-Sunday closing *Carmarthen Journal* to observe:

"This is tightening the rope with a vengeance. We suppose the next thing will be to declare the innkeeper's trade a felony and the innkeeper himself a felon, whom it will be meritorious to catch and hang without benefit of clergy !" (C.J.)

If this seems a strange stand to take in the face of the admitted drink problem in Carmarthen, it should be remembered that although drunken violence was virtually confined to the "labouring classes", drink was a pleasure enjoyed long and often at every level of life in and around the town, and Carmarthen was still the economic and social meeting point for most of them. It was even said that "members of Churches encouraged the illegal drink traffic by allowing their homes to be ' drinking dens ' on the Lord's Day !"[2]

For all Carmarthen's reputation as a drinker's town, though, the problem existed nationwide, but whenever the authorities— local or national—sought to impose controls they met opposition not only from the powerful brewing trade, but also from the masses, for many of whom drink provided the only escape from the realities of a hard life. In Carmarthen in June, 1885, for instance :

> "A ' Demonstration ' on a small scale was got up on the occasion of the defeat of the Government over the Vote of Credit, by which a tax was to be put upon beer and spirits. Mr. Mark's Brass Band were requisitioned, and paraded the town, preceded by a banner on which were the words '*Why rob a poor man of his beer and grog?* ' "
>
> (C.J.)

The ubiquitous Mr. Mark's Brass Band had it made either way ; they were "requisitioned" by both sides—drinkers and temperance workers—whenever they paraded the town to spread their respective gospels !

Tap-room Deserters

It was into this lion's den that the Daniels of the temperance movement made their entrance in the early eighties, though the history of the movement in Carmarthen hardly boded well for them.

In 1882 the temperance movement received a sudden and substantial shot in the arm with the arrival in Carmarthen of the "Blue Ribbon Army", of whom it was said :

> "This movement has made rapid advances in the direction of making people sober since its advent here."
>
> (C.J.)

They brought with them a number of eloquent speakers to proclaim the message, upon which the converted were called forward to take the Pledge, and the large assembly gave fervent voice to the "Blue Ribbon Army's" anthem, the "Doom of Drunkenness" :

> Oppressed with grief Great Britain mourns,
> Her wailings have gone up for years ;
> For sons and daughters daily slain
> She sheds her unavailing tears.

A mourning mother, how she weeps
Because of drunkenness in the land.
The foe that slays her children still,
With rude inexorable hand.

Though famine, plague and war combined
Should boast of millions mown to death,
The Demon Drunkenness grim, alone
Can show more victims of his breath.

And proudly may the Demon point
To the gin palace and hotel
Where his bright poisons are dispensed
With smiles that have a potent spell.

"Am I no licensed fiend ?" says he.
"Have I no legal right to kill ?
Does not my trade support your state ?
I must destroy and slaughter still."

But ah, fell Demon, thou art doomed,
AN ARMY VAST, THE TEMPERANCE HOST
Is forming in the ranks of war
To put an end to thy proud boasts.

It was a frightening message which in the hands of powerful
orators could chill the hearts of even the toughest drunks and
bring them mesmerised, to the rostrum to publicly confess their
evil past and to seek redemption in the Pledge.

And then the great break-through. At a meeting in the Blue
Street Mission Room in November, 1883, the Blue Ribbon
Army produced its prize converts . . . the first of the coraclemen to be netted ! Owen Evans and David Lewis poured out
their repentance in Welsh to the delight of a capacity audience.

The movements multiplied in the town—the Church of
England Temperance Society, the Gospel Temperance Society,
the Carmarthen Total Abstinence Society, the Workingmen's
Temperance Movement, and the Salvation Army. The message
was thundered from the pulpits in packed churches and
chapels :

"'During Lent,' said the Vicar (of St. Peter's), 'we are all called upon to mourn for our personal and individual sins, but to-day we are seriously desired to humble ourselves and mourn for the all-prevailing sin of our Nation, the terrible act of intemperance.

Sober Mahommedans and other heathen nations can point the finger of scorn at our Christianity because of our drunkenness.'" (C. J.)

The Salvation Army commenced its "Bombardment of Carmarthen"[3] in 1885 from its Blue Street "Barracks", led by two doughty females, Captain Annie Banks and Lieutenant Hannah Lees, newcomers to this notorious lair of the Demon Drink. Their distinctively exuberant brand of religion, with its determination not to let the Devil "have all the best tunes",[4] contrasting as it did with the severity of the chapel and the thundering admonitions of its elders and ministers, proved a great attraction to the "lower orders" and the "Barracks" were crowded every evening. One after another the "Tap-room Deserters"—tinworkers, railway engine drivers, street sweepers, quay labourers and coraclemen—ascended the rostrum to proclaim their temperance pledge and their determination not to fall again. At one such meeting—

"Some half dozen of the 'Tap-room Deserters' spoke remarkably well of the evils of intemperance and the blessing of total abstinence, whilst the other portion of the 'Deserters' caused much amusement and merriment by their addresses. One of the latter said that he was the 'father to ten children' (laughter) and alluded to the threats he had received when proclaiming total abstinence on the Quay some time ago. *Notwithstanding the threats of throwing him into the Towy, he yielded not.*"

(C.J.)

Within a few months, the town's temperance bandwagon had rolled to a great climax. Monday the 12th of October, 1885, saw the "Temperance Jubilee" at Carmarthen, when thousands paraded the streets with banners and bands. The railway companies ran excursions at special fares, bringing contingents from the whole of West Wales, and beyond. *And, with the town flooded with people from far and wide, the pubs were packed to the doors* !

Over the next five or six years the various brands of temperance movements achieved varying degrees of success among the hardened drinkers of Carmarthen. A great many of the conversions proved to be "flashes in the pan", as seems to have been the case with—

> "*Our local dipsomaniac.* Daniel Jones (alias ' Danws '), shoemaker, Catherine Street, was sent to gaol for fourteen days for being drunk and disorderly in Catherine Street. Danws' ' Jubilee ' at the police court was long past, this being close on his 60th appearance.
>
> Is there not a Teetotaller in Carmarthen who will try and influence this poor slave to drink to sign the Pledge —*once more* !" (C.J.)

But there is first-hand evidence in the town to this day— nearly a century later—that some had genuinely and permanently "seen the light". More than one member of the old coracle families remembers teetotal, chapel-going grandfathers and great-grandfathers, who in their earlier years had well and truly been members of "that turbulent race" which figured so prominently in the work of the old "Carmarthen Shilling".

In the eighties and nineties, Carmarthen's chapels and churches, their adjoining schoolrooms and the various mission halls scattered throughout the town were packed on most nights of the week for services, temperance meetings, lectures, cymanfa ganu and a variety of cultural entertainments catering for, and attracting, increasingly large congregations and audiences from all classes of the townspeople.

The fact that the temperance movement began to run out of steam in the early nineties in the midst of such a thriving religious life can be attributed on the one hand to the narrowness of its aims, and on the other to the paternalistic—"We know what is good for you"—attitude of its leaders towards those they sought to save. For example, at a Blue Ribbonite meeting, William Spurrell J.P.[5] exhorted the young working men of the town to make use of the Literary and Scientific Institution in the King Street Assembly Rooms, where there was "a large room which ought to be filled and which would help young men to occupy their time well". He regretted the fact that an institution devoted to uplifting young men's minds and to diverting them from coarse pleasure and temptation was not receiving the support it might. But Mr. Spurrell's comments should be read in the light of the fact that it would be another four years before an act of Parliament would reduce the working hours of shop workers under eighteen to a maximum of seventy-four hours a week !

Perhaps "Cosmos" of Cardiff had another answer. Writing under the heading "A Prehistoric Literary Institution" he told how—

> "Some time ago a correspondent of mine visited in Carmarthen the so-called Literary and Scientific Institution of that town. He found a single room presenting many features of almost monastic ascetisism, a fairly liberal supply of newspapers and periodicals, a couple of tables for chess and draughts and a dozen inhospitable wooden chairs.
>
> There was nothing suggestive of science save the extreme severity of the place within and without, and he glanced up at the doorway expecting to see in large, leaden letters some such familiar adaptation of Dante's warning as ' *All levity abandon ye who enter here.*'
>
> How an institution so deplorably antiquated can hope to embrace within its walls anything better than that puritanical fogeydom which loves silence and dull books one is at a loss to understand. A few years since, when some intrepid reformer hinted at billiards and a smoke-room, there arose an agonised outcry in the name of morality and whatnot that fairly froze the reformer's eloquence on his tongue's tip. Since that historic occasion the ice has not been broken and now the apathy of black despair possesses every soul." (C.J.)

The weekly "Workingmen's Temperance" meetings at the Water Street Mission Room in 1891 were now reported to be "sparsely attended", drawing the comment that "Mr. J. F. Morris (the Chairman) deserves greater encouragement in this movement than he now receives, as it has been specially started for the working classes."

The "working classes" of Carmarthen did not seem to know what was good for them !

By February of 1892 it was being said that "The meetings held in connection with the Carmarthen Temperance Society seem to be on the wane these last few weeks, and the late leaders are often conspicuous by their absence." The truth was that the heady excitement, the religious fervour—even mass hysteria —of a packed temperance meeting was not easy to sustain. The "Tap-room Deserters" were objects of curiosity and the centre of attraction as they were paraded—to the amens and hallelujahs of the congregations—to describe the miracle of their conversions. But things looked very different as they left the warmth, the gas light and the adulation of the chapel or mission room and emerged into the dark, narrow streets leading back to the riverside, or to Catherine Street, Water Street, Woods Row, Cambrian Place, Priory Street or wherever their damp dark and overcrowded little cottages were. Things hadn't changed there ; life was no easier, nor was it easy to endure the ridicule of their fellows. And there was always a pub and another solacing drink within arm's reach !

Whatever its weaknesses, though, and whatever its miscalculations of the mood or aspirations of the "labouring classes", the temperance movement in Carmarthen made a number of more or less permanent, more or less total, conversions among the hard-core of the town's drunks. And that was not all. Throughout the nation (incidentally "Through Darkest England" was one of the most popular of the temperance lectures) the movement stirred consciences to the point where Parliament passed new licensing regulations and local magistrates seized the opportunities they gave for a reduction in the numbers of licensed houses.

The "War" of the Blue Ribbonites' Marching Song would be fought long and hard in Carmarthen for many years yet, and the place would never lose its reputation as a drinker's town, but the temperance movement of the eighties and nineties deserves a great deal of the credit for the removal of the worst excesses of its drunkenness by the century's end.

NOTES

1See later the town ministers' criticism of the practice of giving drink to curry the voters' favour.

2A temperance worker quoted in the *Carmarthen Journal*.

3This and the term "Barracks" were used by a correspondent to the *Carmarthen Journal*.

4The founder of the Salvation Army, William Booth, is said to have asked "Why should the Devil have all the best tunes?"

5Author of the most useful, and now rare, history-cum-guidebook of Carmarthen, published in 1879.

CHAPTER ELEVEN

CARMARTHEN'S PRIDE

Tuesday the 22nd of June, 1897, dawned in Carmarthen "amid an occasional powdering of small rain", and few but the night men of the "Carmarthen Shilling" were awake and present to witness when, at five o'clock, the silence over the old town was shattered by a bugle call, sounded to all quarters of Guildhall Square by David Rees, the "Official Bugler".[1] The martial opening of the day provided by Bugler Rees was maintained when, at eight o'clock, a cannon boomed from Penlan Hill, the first shot in a cannonade that was sustained with but short pauses for the next seventeen hours ! And as the echoes of the first salvo rattled around the narrow streets of the town, the bells of Saint Peter added their message.

Carmarthen was about to celebrate Queen Victoria's Diamond Jubilee—"Sixty Glorious Years" that had brought the nation to its highest point of achievement as an industrial power second to none and the centre of the greatest empire ever known.

Pride burned no more fiercely anywhere in the Kingdom than in the hearts of the people of Carmarthen, who would enter into the spirit of the event with every ounce of their customary enthusiasm and verve. All classes of the town would come together for the heady thrill of belonging to the most powerful nation on earth.

The town was decorated as never before and a huge procession paraded the streets, behind bands, banners and marching men of Carmarthen's own redcoats, the 1st Volunteer Battalion of the Welsh Regiment. Prominent in the procession was one of the best-known figures in town—burly, bearded Thomas Smith, head of the "Carmarthen Shilling" and Chief of the Fire Brigade. Behind him, "looking very brave", fire-axes hanging from broad belts on heavy black jackets, brass helmets gleaming in the morning sun, marched the firemen.

186

And then came Carmarthen's Pride—the "Carmarthen Shilling"—two of whom held pride of place in the procession . . . next to the Mayor, of course. Sergeant John Harries shouldered the Corporation Mace and Constable No. 4 Thomas Davies, ex farmer's boy from Llanarthne, exercised a privilege unique to Carmarthen—that of carrying the Corporation Sword before the Mayor, Mr. H. Brunel White. For three hundred and fifty years Carmarthen had been (as it still is) the only town in Wales allowed this signal honour, an honour bestowed by King Henry the Eighth in 1546 when he ordered that ". . . a Sword-bearer of the Mayor shall freely and lawfully carry the sword before the said Mayor, in the manner as is accustomed to be done in our City of London." The honour of carrying the sword in procession always went to a policeman of the "Carmarthen Shilling" until the force ceased to exist in 1947. No policeman has carried it since.

And there was a special symbolism in the choice of rearguard for the procession—half a dozen coraclemen carrying their craft over their backs as their forefathers had carried theirs since the time when Carmarthen was a tiny Celtic settlement, before the Romans came.

As the procession arrived in the square, the Mayor, his Corporation and various of the town worthies took up their positions on the Guildhall steps, and the band and the Volunteers formed ranks in open order. The square was packed and every window overlooking it filled with spectators as twelve o'clock struck and Captain Holmes' order roared above the din of the crowd : "Volunteers—load—present—fire !" and rifles cracked their "feu de joie" and filled the square with smoke. The band struck up the National Anthem and Captain Holmes' parade-ground voice roared again "Volunteers—load —present—fire", for the final volley. And then, before the smoke of the firing had cleared, Mrs. D. J. Thomas "amidst a death-like stillness" commenced to sing God Save The Queen, in which she was joined by the large choir assembled there. There were then three cheers for the Queen from the huge crowd, who, with the choir, gave a "hearty rendering" of All People That On Earth Do Dwell.

The afternoon was occupied by "Rustic Sports" in Mr. Bowen's field behind the Railway Tavern at the top end of Lammas Street. The field was packed and the Volunteer Band provided a musical accompaniment to a programme of sports and games in which all classes of the townspeople took part. The schoolchildren were entertained at tea parties in their respective schools and given a commemoration medal each, while the "indoor paupers" of the workhouse received a welcome respite from their stonebreaking and other "honest toil" and from their normally drab lifestyle in recognition of the occasion.

In the evening the Market Place was filled to overflowing for a "Promenade Concert", but it was really too much to expect on such a day as this, with the pubs open and packed to the doors right through the day from early morning, that the audience would be one hundred per cent attentive. The event began to fall apart from the outset as the excited and largely tipsy crowd "entertained itself in various ways, some of the singers absolutely failing to obtain a hearing, owing to the disorder among the audience !"[2]

The final blow to the performers at the promenade concert came when the cannons fired another salvo from Penlan Hill and a number of fire balloons rose into the air, the signal for a mass exodus from the Market Place as the crowds made their way—like good soldiers—towards the sound of the guns. There was a huge bonfire on Penlan and even the crowded pubs emptied—momentarily—for the spectacular blaze, while those up there argued as to whether ten, a dozen or even two dozen bonfires could be seen on the surrounding hills.

When the fire was well alight the crowd sang the National Anthem for the umpteenth time, and gave three cheers for their Queen, at which moment someone shouted that the town pubs had been granted an extension of hours. And the bonfire was all but deserted as quickly as the Market Place had been emptied !

The "Carmarthen Shilling" were well in evidence all through the day and in every part of town, but for all the massive drinking spree that accompanied the day's celebrations, and for all the skirmishes they put down and family quarrels they quiet-

"Pride burned no more fiercely anywhere in the Kingdom than in the hearts of the people of Carmarthen" P. C. Davies, the Sword Bearer, stands by the left centre column, with Sgt. Harries, the Mace Bearer, just in front of him

David Jones ". . . would, by dint of hard work, loyalty and the respect he gained from his colleagues and from all classes of the town, become the 'Shilling's' first Inspector, and deputy to his chief"

". . . that veteran old tramp, S.S. 'Merthyr', unloading yet another cargo of flour alongside J. B. Arthur's quayside warehouse"

Carmarthen Quay in 1895

The S.S. 'Merthyr' leaves for Bristol at the turn of the century

Sergeant John Harries, veteran of thirty-two years service, worthy successor in the rank to David Williams

FAIR IN CARMARTHEN.

" . . . there was still room in the town for the ancient street markets like the Gas Lane Cattle market"
(Gas Lane is now called Morfa Lane, and it is lined on the right by terraced houses, while the pointed top of the church tower has gone. The park railings are on the left of the lane)

". . . the October Priory Street Fair . . . a very large fair, much frequented by a considerable number of dealers from England on the lookout for young horses"

"Lammas Street, too, would be filled with horses, cattle, carriages, haggling farmers and dealers and drunks when its own ancient fair day came around"

Saint Peter's Church at the turn of the century

The Monument to Major General Sir William Nott, G.C.B., erected in 1851 in
the old market place, renamed in his honour 'Nott Square'

ened, not one drunk had to be locked up. All of them got home somehow, although many of them "hadn't a leg under them", and the day ended—at least for most—by one o'clock in the morning when "the bonfire had practically burnt itself out and the town had gone to sleep, with the exception of one or two back streets where some private family matters were being discussed in a very public and emphatic manner !"[3]

Thus had the people of Carmarthen celebrated their country's arrival at the high point of Empire.

POACHER TURNED GAMEKEEPER

Among the many hundreds of people who had come from far afield to join in the Carmarthen celebrations was a young Cardiganshire lad, David Jones, and travelling home to Newcastle Emlyn on the late excursion train he reflected on the sights and sounds of the day—the flags, the music, the procession, the cannons, the sports, the bonfire. And he carried with him a vivid memory of the "Carmarthen Shilling" marching behind their bearded chief, dispersing themselves around the packed square, mingling with the revellers in the crowded streets and pubs, curbing the excesses of the wilder elements and giving a helping hand to those who hadn't a leg under them.

And on that day the seeds of an ambition were sown in David Jones's mind, an ambition that would bring him back to Carmarthen less than a year later.

This twenty-five year old gamekeeper from Colonel Prior's Cardiganshire estate came highly recommended by his employer and the local magistrates . . . which, some say, was the only way they could think of to be rid of the best poacher in Cardiganshire ! At all events, as a Sergeant in the "Carmarthen Shilling" he was able to teach his Chief Constable a thing or two about salmon and trout fishing and other country crafts, and he would share the secret of the illegal fishing net seized by the "Shilling" from salmon poachers and kept in the station property store for years after other contemporary items had been disposed of. They say it saw the river again. More than once !

David Jones would also, by dint of **hard** work, loyalty and the respect he gained from his colleagues and from all classes of the town, become the "Shilling's" first Inspector and deputy to his chief. He would see the "Shilling" over the threshold of the century and serve until 1929, remaining in Carmarthen in his retirement and dying in 1946 . . . the year in which the government decreed by Act of Parliament that police forces like Carmarthen's had no place in a world that had decided that "big is beautiful".

He stepped from the train at Carmarthen Town Station that April morning in 1898 and walked into town, pausing halfway over the river bridge to take in the jumble of buildings that lay between the town centre and the river, looking as if they had simply spilled and strewn down the steep, crowded hillside—only just falling short of tumbling into the Towy. He contemplated, too, the ships tied up along the quay and anchored in the river . . . the schooner ' Charles ' of Dublin, the ketch ' Falcon ' of Plymouth, the ill-fated ' Tivyside ' of Liverpool,[4] and that veteran old tramp the s.s. ' Merthyr ', unloading yet another cargo of flour alongside J. B. Arthur's quayside warehouse . . . some of the dozen or so vessels like the steamers ' Turtle ', ' Teale ', ' King Ja Ja ', ' Ant ' and ' Dunvegan ' that still linked Bristol, Cardiff, Swansea, Ireland, North Wales and Liverpool with Carmarthen. The old port was still forty years away from extinction.

He watched the carts trundling off the quay and saw those headed for Spilman Street being reinforced by Mr. Bland's trace-horses for the steep pull up Castle Hill. And then he walked up to the town, through narrow climbing Bridge Street, and past its many pubs—the ' Red Cow ', the ' Pelican ', the ' Wheat Sheaf ', the ' Railway ', the ' Horse & Jockey ' and the ' Buffalo ', all of which would feel his heavy tread over the years to come.[5] Emerging into Nott Square, by the ' Angel Vaults ', he was almost in the heart of the old town, in a tiny area crammed with shops and shoppers as far as the eye could see before King Street bent away from view beyond the still elegant face of the old Assembly Rooms.[6]

And so to the Guildhall. It was an honour indeed to be appointed to the Carmarthen Borough Police, for Mayor H.

Brunel White and his fellow Watch Committee members could afford to be choosy, given the long waiting list for the now rare vacancies in the force, and this healthy country lad looked just the kind to handle himself well among the fighting drunks of Mill Street, Catherine Street and the riverside.[7] So, with an extra spring in his step, David Jones followed Sergeant John Harries on the 230 yards walk from the Guildhall to the spot from where Carmarthen had been "watched" and policed for almost a century—the Cambrian Place Station House.

What stories could be told about this spot, where even at the century's end the station house windows were provided with iron shutters which were clanged shut against the besieging mob whenever a drunk was dragged screaming and kicking through its doorway. Those shutters would be needed for many years yet.

For David Jones that station house would p‹vide a personal and bitter memory. He would become the resident station house keeper, his wife would bear her children there, and its all-pervading dampness would be the death of her.

Over the months that followed, David Jones savoured to the full the sights and sounds and smells that characterised Carmarthen at the close of the 19th century. He patrolled the crowded provision and livestock markets, keeping the drunken farmers in some kind of order, regulating the "cheap-jacks" and prosecuting those who shouted their wares, squeezing through the busy narrow spaces between the stalls which crowded around the marvellous Italianate clock-tower, centre-piece of Carmarthen's famous fifty-year old market. The Roman-numeralled clocks on the tower showed the correct time to all quarters of the bustling market, as they had ever since 1846 . . . but the 20th century would cure that, leaving unmoving hands and neglected stonework as just one more piece of evidence of the town's forgetfulness of its past.[8]

Only the width of a street—and the open doors of the Tanners' Arms[9] heaving with drovers, farmers and dealers—separated the provision market from the largest livestock mart in the Principality, the throbbing heart of Carmarthenshire's agricultural prosperity. Large as it was, though, there was still room in the town for the ancient street marts, like the Gas

Lane cattle market, the Lammas Street horse fair and, biggest of all, the October Priory Street Fair. Here the policemen squeezed past the many groups of farmers, leaning on their blackthorns, glasses in hand, sealing deals with the spit and slap of their palms on the pavements outside half a dozen pubs. Many things had changed, but not the Priory Street Fairs.

Nor the ancient Church of Saint Peter nearby—the soul of Carmarthen, the scene of so many thanksgivings and cele-bratory prayers for victories, for deliverance from plague and epidemic, for new monarchs and for new mayors. Saint Peter's, whose tower had heard the screams and shouts of the Blue mob of 1831 and whose old sexton had fought bravely but in vain to save the flag ; Saint Peter's, where old General Nott had been laid to rest after wearing himself out in his country's service in India ;[10] Saint Peter's whose name was (and is) proudly borne by native born Carmarthen men—"Saint Peter's Boys"— scattered throughout the world, and whose solid fabric had watched over seven hundred years of life in this still tiny town.

From the church, the policemen walked their beats past the Georgian facade of Furnace House, where the town's other hero, General Sir Thomas Picton had sworn death or glory before leaving to meet his death at Waterloo more than eighty years before. And crossing the narrow top of Little Water Street and into King Street, they brushed by the ' Marquis of Granby ', where long-dead Nicholas Martin had committed his first disciplinary offence of "being found tippling" sixty years before—the first of at least forty four such infractions ! And a few yards on, beyond the corner of Queen Street, where Mr. Collard's ' Queen's Hotel ' was renowned for its twopenny (less than 1p) sleever of Draught Bass,[11] they would see the com-manding figure of General Nott gazing out towards them from his pedestal, over a multitude of shop blinds.[12] The old "Sepoy General" still surveyed the square named for him fifty years before.

Down through Hall Street, or through even narrower Saint Mary Street, and they were in Guildhall Square, the heart of the old town as Saint Peter's is its soul. Could they perhaps hear faint echoes of the clamour of 1831, the quick-marching feet of the Militiamen, the steely swish of bayonets drawn from scabbards, the clatter of cavalry hooves charging to the rescue of a rash, mob-threatened, new-broom chief constable of over half a century ago ? Guildhall Square—yet to receive its monument to the Carmarthenshire men who would soon find their graves fighting the Boer in South Africa—was peaceful now, but an aura of history pervaded the Square and its Georgian hall, which had acted like magnets for generations of the townspeople whenever word spread of an event that called for the kind of celebration at which Carmarthen excelled.

The square would soon be filled for the farewells to the volunteer Saint Peter's Boys off to fight the Boer and for the celebrations attending the reliefs of Ladysmith and Mafeking, but it would not see any more rioters, or Militia bayonets, or Dragoons, or "London Thief-takers", or any but the "Carmarthen Shilling", for the only skirmishes this square would see would involve a diminishing band of "Old Offenders" and those visitors from the scattered villages whose weekly "spree" robbed them of their legs and their senses.

Below the square, Dark Gate was still narrow, and one could always find a member of the "Carmarthen Shilling" there, hands behind back, beard tucked in above pouting, silver-buttoned belly, ready to direct the stranger, admonish or arrest the drunk, or to chase the ubiquitous "furious rider". If he thought he had his hands full with town and country drunks, he might reflect that there were still buildings around Dark Gate whose walls had heard the frenzied cries of the Carmarthen Mob as they pelted John Jones of Ystrad, scattered John Lazenby's bruised and battered "London Thief-takers", and pulled Richard Rees from his horse and beat him into near insensibility . . . seventy years before.

As the policemen walked on, Lammas Street broadened out dramatically from narrow Dark Gate, and it, too would be filled with horses, cattle, carriages, haggling farmers and dealers and drunks when its own ancient fair day came around. But what would always strike them as they walked up past the ' Boar's Head Hotel '—the last of the town's coaching inns, scene of fashionable balls, celebratory dinners, and after-hours drinking by the town worthies for well over a century—was the "Fusiliers' Monument" and the great iron-wheeled Russian cannon alongside it, down whose barrel the blue-clad arms of the "Carmarthen Shilling" were thrust each night to find the bottles of ale left for them by obliging publicans !

The obelisk, a unique memorial to the dead of the Crimean war and the many battle honours of the 23rd Regiment, the Royal Welsh Fusiliers, had been refurbished by public subscription nearly forty years before, when the Alma, Inkerman. Balaclava and Sebastopol were still well within living memory. And now the names on the memorial were beginning to fade again. Come the 20th century and the dead of the Crimea, whose graves were nearly two thousand miles away from their Welsh homeland and whose names would be all but weathered away, might well wonder if Carmarthen had ceased to care altogether.

But on through the town, and away from the main streets to the places where David Jones could expect to find much of his evening and week-end work—in Water Street, Goose Street, Catherine Street, Woods Row, Blue Street and the narrow winding streets and steps around the quay and the bridge. And, of course, the battleground of Cambrian Place, where James Davies, alias Jim Bach y Square, regularly raised the roof on Saturday nights and old Mary Daniel, alternately roaring, singing and crying in her cups, was wont to hammer on the station house door demanding to be locked up.

The few yards from Mill Street and Shaws Lane to the Cambrian Place lock-up was a well-worn path along which Jack the Tinman, Twm Lodging House, Jones the Dormouse and any of a dozen of the drunks from "the lowest courts and alleys of Carmarthen"[13] featured in week-end battles as the policemen struggled to drag them to the cells, while their neighbours— worthy descendants of the old "Carmarthen Mob"—fought just as furiously to rescue them.

Hence the iron shutters over the station house windows !

And then there were the lodging houses to be visited, to see that their over-generous quotas were not exceeded. Ada Thompson's on Dan y Banc—still a notoriously rough quarter —could always be counted on to house a surfeit of tramps, drunks and ragged women and children and so qualify her for a trip to the magistrates' court, while Ada herself could fight as hard as any man when the gin took her. She was a worthy successor to Annie Awberry—she of the hundred and odd convictions !

There was, too, all the other daily routine of police work, and as the season came around the "Shilling" would be present in force at the agricultural shows and the races, where the beer tents would be heaving. John Arthur was not the last of the "Carmarthen Shilling" to come to grief through the generosity of the show-ground beer-sellers.

In the winter, when the poor were poorer and the hungry were hungrier, Carmarthen's policemen helped out at the soup kitchens, where bowls of "Wholesome broth" and loaves of bread donated by the charitable were doled out to ragged parents and barefoot children. The station house itself would house a soup kitchen when the winter was particularly harsh or unemployment was particularly rife, but the town's policemen were responsive at all times to the distress of their poor neighbours. David Jones would often put his skill as a tailor to good use for the needs of the poor children around Cambrian Place ; he made many a pair of short trousers out of old police uniforms.

Yes, it was a full life for a member of the "Carmarthen Shilling" and when he could find nothing better to do he could always spend half an hour at the corner of narrow Dark Gate— the hub of the town through which everyone passed sooner or later—and the policeman at Dark Gate could stand and watch the world go by, much as his successors do to this day. One could say—with appropriate diffidence, of course—that it was Carmarthen's equivalent of Piccadilly Circus, the hub of a rather larger town a couple of hundred miles to the east.

David Jones, poacher turned gamekeeper, would have been a rich man if he had had a pound for every hour he spent watching the world go by Dark Gate over the next thirty-one years.

All in all, then, the "Carmarthen Shilling" kept a tidy town as they walked the seven miles of "streets, alleys and roads" and "watched" the town's 2,082 houses.[14] They were known to everybody and were quick to spot the stranger ; they kept the town's urchins in line with the occasional cuff behind the ear, and they had resort to the courts only when their own brand of

195

summary justice or a sternly delivered "gipsy's warning" failed to do the trick.

These men epitomised an age and art of policing as far removed from the mobile policeman as the art of conversation is removed from the silence-inducing television set in the living room corner. And society is the poorer for the loss of it.

ANOTHER GOLDEN DAWN

And so to the century's end. What should be Chief Constable Smith's strategy for New Year's Eve, 1900, the night that would mark the end of the 19th century and the beginning of the 20th. Would it explode in the old traditional manner ? Would the exuberant and exciteable townspeople revive the long-dead "Torchnight"—the blazing tar barrels, the flaming torches, the fireworks and the gunfire—to mark the coming of a new century that, so they were told on all hands, promised so much in scientific advance and in man's progress towards Utopia ?

"Better safe than sorry" said Mayor Spurrell, so the orders were given and the "Shilling" was out in full twelve-strong force as the streets and pubs began to fill, that Monday evening. To us who have observed the manner in which the birth of the 19th century was greeted in Carmarthen, the pattern that was now taking shape is familiar, and there would be much drunken carousing before morning brought the new century.

But there was a difference. There were other crowded places. All the chapels and all the churches were filled as the hour approached. Water Street Chapel (Capel Heol Dŵr) was filled to its capacity of 900 for the meeting of the Carmarthen Total Abstinence Society, at which the children of the Mill Street Mission sang heartily in their "Sunday Best". The Salvation Army Citadel in Blue Street was packed, and among the band, playing the bass drum, was Wil y Dŵr[15]—water inspector, fire brigade auxilliary, coracleman . . . and poacher. Typical of the coraclemen who had responded to the religious and temperance influence of the Salvation Army, Wil y Dŵr had been so deeply moved as to sign the pledge, to preach regularly in

196

"The Old 'Sepoy General' still surveyed the square named for him fifty years before"
(Nott Square at the turn of the century)

"Guildhall Square, the heart of the old town . . . was peaceful now" (Pictured at
the turn of the century, before the Boer War memorial was placed before the
Guildhall)

"The Boar's Head Hotel (Lammas Street)—the last of the town's coaching inns, scene of fashionable balls, celebratory dinners, and after hours drinking by the town's worthies . . ."

Lammas Street, looking towards Dark Gate, early in the twentieth century

The *Welshman* newspaper office in Lammas Street, 1898

The Fusilier Monument in the 1890s

. . . and after the turn of the century

River Towy and Quay

CARMARTHEN

"The neighbourhood of the Quay . . . noted for quarrels between husbands and wives"

". . . the policemen at Dark Gate could stand and watch the world go by . . ."
(P.C. No. 9 William Jones Rees, who joined in 1907 and retired in 1933)

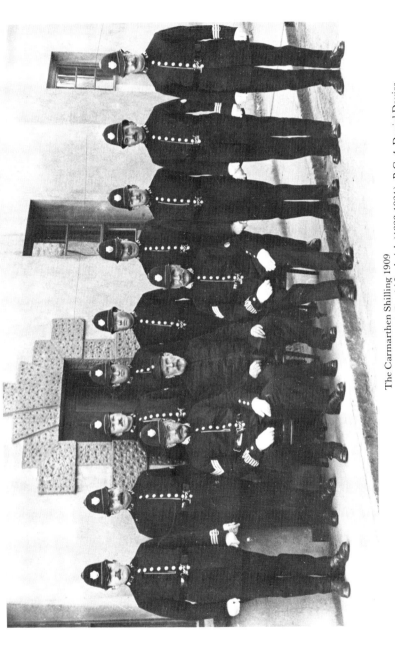

The Carmarthen Shilling 1909

Left to right: P.C. 7 John Walters (1907-1932); P.C. 5 David Lodwick (1888-1921); P.C. 4 Daniel Davies
(1903-1930); P.C. 3 William Llewellyn (1903-1930); P.C. 8 William Davies (1899-1921); P.C. 1 David Jones
(1898-1929); P.C. 9 William Jones Rees (1907-1933); P.C. 2 Thomas Rees (1903-1911); P.C. 6 John Daniel Williams (1908-1934)
.... Thomas Davies (1878-1911)

Guildhall Square, and—even more significantly for him—to temper his poaching activities. He now resolutely refrained from going out with his salmon poacher's net until the midnight hour signalled the passing of the Lord's Day !

Everyone in town was celebrating in his or her own way. The 'Boar's Head Hotel' was host to the "Military and Fancy Dress Ball" of the 1st Volunteer Battalion, The Welsh Regiment, and on the other side of town the windows of the Church of Saint Peter glowed with light and song as the vicar and his congregation celebrated their customary Welsh Service, a service that ended with the traditional New Year gift of bread to the aged poor of the Parish, while all around the town the people prayed, or sang, or drank, or talked of the "Good Old Days".

And in the very heart of Carmarthen, Guildhall Square beckoned to its townspeople. No prior announcement was needed, nor advertisement, nor any invitation. Only the unspoken, time-honoured feeling that that was the place to be. There were plenty of drunks and revellers about the place—but there were no fireworks, no blazing tar barrels, no torches, no cracking pistols . . . and no prisoners for the lock-up . . . as the bells of Saint Peter chimed in the new century and another golden dawn.

The only explosion in the packed Guildhall Square at the midnight hour was an explosion of song.

What a difference a century had made. Just one hundred years before, old Wil y Lôn had shuffled his way through a tiny, dark town of which only the very centre saw the faint glimmer of oil lamps, doing his best to steer clear of the fighting mobs of drunks, and disappearing altogether into the comparative safety of his little "Watch box" when the pistols and fowling pieces began to fire on New Year's Eve and other nights of special exuberance in an almost lawless town.

But at midnight on the last day of the 19th century, his burly, well-respected (or feared, as occasion demanded) successors, the "Carmarthen Shilling", stood fearless and friendly guard over a brightly gas-lit Guildhall Square, surrounded by electric lighted shop windows, joining in with the choir and their fellow townspeople in their hymns to the coming century.

So, for all this, had Carmarthen been tamed ? Well . . . let us say "nearly". It was no longer "the most turbulent town in Wales" and the days had gone when people stood in awe at Carmarthen's reputation for violence. And yet, as the 19th century came to its close, there was still something of the "frontier" town about Carmarthen ; still something "different" about the place.

In the years to come, those who governed the town would eventually destroy much of its shape and architectural character in their anxiety to conform, but those influences of the 20th century that have moulded others into dull conformity would never tame its people's independent spirit and sense of fun.

When was it, for example, that Carmarthen added to its election folk-lore the singing of Welsh hymns by a vast and excited crowd awaiting an election result in the early hours of the morning—singing conducted from the window of the Mayor's office in Nott Square by the chief of the town's police ? Not in 1850, not in 1900 . . . but in 1974 !

And when was it that while the Mayor and his entourage were refreshing themselves in the ' Jolly Tar ' by the Quay steps, some joker pulled the plug on the Mayoral barge, causing it to sink as they boarded it for the ceremonial voyage of the Mayor—the Admiral of the Port of Carmarthen—down to the Towy estuary in exercise of his ancient jurisdiction ?[16] Not in 1800, when Carmarthen Port was at its busiest, nor in 1900 when steamers still lined its quay. No. It was in 1971 !

And Christmas Eve in Carmarthen is still "different", for while there may not now be any blazing tar barrels or pistol-firing horsemen, it is only the absence of horses and carriages, gas lamps and earthen streets that disturbs the illusion that "Torchnight" is of but recent memory.

While the people of Carmarthen are as honest and industrious as ever and the town still maintains the educational and religious excellence of which it has for long been rightly proud, one has only to join the farmers and dealers and their families on "Mart" day, or the shoppers in the provision market, or the thousands who flock to the County Show, to find another answer to the question "Had Carmarthen been tamed ?" For one thing, it is one of the few places (if not the only place) where pubs are open through the day most days of the week, a long and continuing tradition recognised as long ago as the sixteenth century when King Henry the Eighth enshrined it in a Royal Charter.[17] Deals are still sealed in the 'Ceffyl Du' (the Black Horse), the 'Tanners' Arms', the 'Weavers' and the 'Mansel Arms' and the other pubs surrounding the markets and marts, just as they were a hundred years ago.

Now, as then, such days end on a note of happy exhaustion, for Carmarthen is still "Mine Host" to thousands.

No, Carmarthen would never be "tamed" ; never for so long as its people retained their sense of fun, their lack of inhibition and their gregariousness, and for so long as it produced—as it still produces—the friendly, convivial and unpredictable "characters" from all walks of life for which the town is still famed over a great part of Wales.

There is a vast store of tales about Carmarthen's twentieth-century "characters" and their escapades, but—chwarateg—a respect for those concerned, living and dead, suggests that the telling of them should be left to a later generation.

Towns, like people, are products of their past. Why else has Carmarthen a reputation for being a town that is really a large village, a town that still has one foot in an age when people were far more gregarious, far more hospitable, far more neighbourly, far less inhibited and far more convivial ? The ships may have gone and the river may be empty, and life in the old town is rather less colourful and exuberant, yet the distinctive flavour of Old Carmarthen is still there.

Carmarthen IS a "different" town.

Perhaps one day the rest of the world will get in step.

As for the "Shilling", it is but a memory now. Those early guardians of the law whose antics and exploits have run as a constant—if often erratic—thread through this story, are all but forgotten. The foundations of the "Roundhouse", the station house and the borough gaol lie beneath yet another supermarket.

But though police forces to-day have much to boast of in the way of methods and resources, we should never forget that the foundation for all that they have was laid by men like the "Carmarthen Shilling"—wayward, hard to handle and no less drunken than those from whom they were drawn[18]—men throughout the land who created, sustained against all the assaults of a hostile populace, and presented to the 20th century, the substance of a police system second to none in the world.

Let that be their memorial.

NOTES

[1]It was said of David Rees that "he continued throughout the day to bugle in such a thoroughly efficient manner that if he lives to see the next Jubilee, the duty of Official Bugler will undoubtedly fall to his lot on that occasion." (C.J.)

[2]*Carmarthen Journal.*

[3]*Carmarthen Journal.*

[4]The 'Tivyside', a 130-ton steamer, went onto the rocks off the Gower near Port Eynon on the night of 14th June 1900 and was totally wrecked, but with no loss of life. Several Carmarthen men on a pleasure trip spent the night in an open boat before reaching shore—and returning home to Carmarthen by train.

[5]They have all gone now, but the words 'Red Cow' in fading red paint can still be discerned on the wall of the end house which overlooks Coracle Way, the 3-lane highway which has obliterated everything that lay between the town and the Quay.

[6]In another act of 20th century vandalism, the elegant facade was covered with a featureless cement rendering. The building now houses a cinema.

[7]Right to the end of the force's existence (in 1947) Carmarthen needed big men who were prepared to stand up and fight—man to man—when reason failed. On 31st March, 1947, the average height of Carmarthen's borough policemen was six feet.

[8]Shortly after this book went to publication work began on restoring the clock tower as part of the modernisation of the market.

[9]Still as busy in 1980!

[10]William Nott, whose father kept the Ivy Bush coaching inn in King Street, left Carmarthen in 1800 at the age of 18 to serve with the army of the Honourable East India Company. He returned 44 years later to a hero's welcome, as befitted the man most responsible for the defeat of the Afghans and for avenging the massacre of the British army in its retreat from Kabul in 1842. He was dead within three months of his return home.

[11]The "Queen's" is still renowned for the quality of its draught Bass, though, sadly, it now costs considerably more than 1p a pint!

[12]The statue was cast from the bronze of a cannon captured at the battle of Maharajpur and donated by the Honourable East India Company.

[13]*Carmarthen Journal.*

[14]Report of Her Majesty's Inspector of Constabulary, 1900.

[15]William Thomas, Inspector of the town's water supply and member of the old coracle family of Thomases. It was said that there were no reliable records of the locations of the town's water mains and that Wil y Dŵr (Wil the Water) carried them all in his head and shared his secrets with no one. The truth of this became evident in the years after his death. There was utter confusion!

[16]The now titular office of Admiral is held under King Henry VIII's Charter of 1546, and the Mayor carries a silver oar as his emblem. His court had the duty of preventing obstructions in the river, and it is ironic that the replacement boat for this Mayor's voyage ran aground on a gravel bank—one of the "obstructions" which the Royal Charter required him, as Admiral, to prevent!

[17]The *Western Mail* of 20th April, 1977, headlined a generous extension by the town magistrates for over 100 pubs in what the newspaper termed a "Welsh drinkers' paradise", a comment that evoked a storm of protest, principally from the town's Ministers of Religion.

[18]In the first two years (1829-1831) of its existence, the London Metropolitan Police lost around 2,000 men, of whom some 80% were dismissed for drunkenness. Carmarthen's proportion of loss through drink was a steady 90% . . . over its first ten years. Let Carmarthen take comfort from the fact that that—give or take a percent—was no worse than the figure for any police force in the Kingdom.

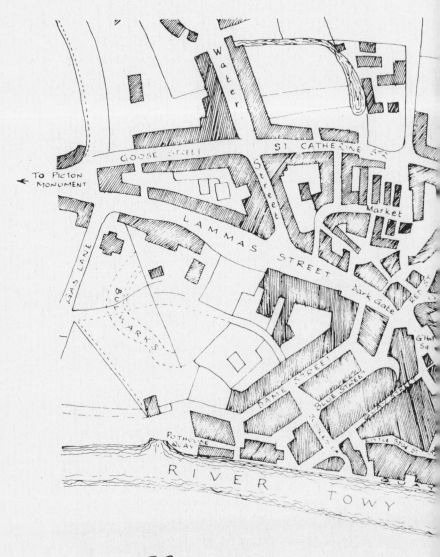

To Picton
Monument

Water Street

Goose Street

St Catherine Str

Street

Market

Lammas Street

Dark Gate

Agas Lane

Bulwarks

G'Hall
Sa

Dame Street

Blue Street

Pothouse
Clay

River

Towy

Carmarthen c. 1879

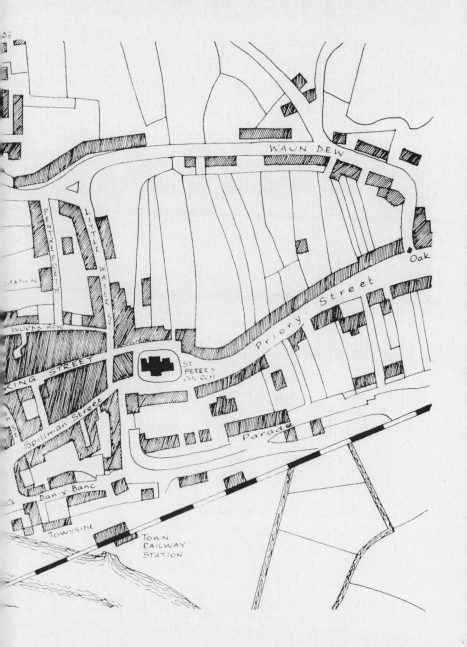

WAUN DEW

PENTRE POETH

LITTLE WATER ST.

STATION

WOODS ROW

Oak

Priory Street

KING STREET

ST PETERS CHURCH

Spillman Street

Parade

Dan·y·Banc

TOWYSIDE

TOWN RAILWAY STATION

PAT. MOLLOY 1979